Also by Michael Keene

BOOKS

Folklore and Legends of Rochester

Murder, Mayhem & Madness

Mad House

Abandoned

FILMS

The Murder of William Lyman

The Strange Disappearance of Captain William Morgan

In Search of White Crows

The Code of Handsome Lake

Visions

Question of Sanity

The True Story of Female Serial Killers in 19th Century New York

MICHAEL T. KEENE

WM

Published by Willow Manor Publishing

Fredericksburg, V.A. 22406

www.willowmanorpublishing.com

First published 2015

Manufactured in the United States

LCCN 2015931908

Library of Congress Catalogue-in-Publication Data

Keene, Michael.

Question of Sanity: The True Story of Female Serial Killers
in 19th Century New York

Michael Keene

p.cm.

Includes bibliographical references.

ISBN 978-1-939688-21-7

1.History—New York (state). 2. Crime—New York (state). 3.Female Serial Killers—New York
(state). 4. 19th Century—New York (state). 5. Women—New York (state).

Anecdotes. I. Title

Contents

Introduction

In my previous book, *Abandoned*, I explored the untold story of orphan asylums and the role their development played in the establishment of the Orphan Train Movement. My initial research brought me to the streets of New York City and pointed me towards the contributions of key people in the orphanage movement such as Lewis M. Pease, Charles Loring Brace and Sister Irene Fitzgibbon. While I found their own personal stories fascinating, as well as their generosity and empathy for children, a story behind the story grabbed my attention and that story was the role of mothers contributing to the homelessness of their own children.

Traditionally and culturally, we are inclined to presume upon the maternal instinct of women. We believe that it is a membership of our society that is innately nurturing, and if pushed to choose between their own welfare and that of their loved ones—and children, especially—that mothers will sacrifice in favor of the latter.

However, significant evidence during the mid-1800s proved that this was clearly not the case. In fact, by the end of the Civil War studies estimated that the streets of New York harbored more than 30,000 homeless children, the majority of which were abandoned by their parents. Children old enough to fend for themselves slept in alleyways and door fronts, resorting to petty crime or selling newspapers and buttons for meal money. Desperate mothers left Infants on the doorsteps outside missions and churches.

Based on this willingness to discard one's own children, I felt curious to see just how far this contrary behavior might extend. But I wanted a historical perspective. So I set out to research the most heinous and murderous activity attributed to women belonging to the 19th century and residing within New York State. To narrow the field, I sought to include only those women accused of being serial killers.

The Concept of Serial Killings

A murderer must kill at least three people, all within proximity to each other in terms of time, in order to be formally classified as a serial killer. It is generally accepted that serial killers are pattern killers. The motive is the same one murder to the next, as is the means by which the deaths are brought about.

Over 90% of serial killers are men between the ages of 20 and 30. Experts believe most suffered some sort of emotional scarring as a child, often at the hand of a parent, a trusted relative or family friend, often the result of physical or sexual abuse. As these children enter their teen years, at the stage of development where such thoughts become possible, they tend to exist in a make-believe world of psycho-sexual fantasy which progresses with age to actual acts of violence. The murders they commit are usually motivated by deep psychological issues that defy rational explanation.

Male serial killers tend to fall into two categories: organized and disorganized. Organized killers show IQs above normal, produce a higher quantity of kills, and plan the kill down to the smallest detail. They are less likely to leave behind evidence and kidnap, kill and discard the body all in different places. Rape and torture are often performed as a means of self-gratification. The disorganized killer is spontaneous and of lower intelligence. He takes advantage of the moment to select his victim and uses whatever is available to commit the murder. This murderer doesn't move the body from its place of death. There is no rape or torture; however, many times the killer takes a souvenir.

In addition, there is scientific evidence supporting the theory that serial killers tend to possess areas of the brain involved in emotional response, such as the amygdala or other parts of the limbic system, which are physically underdeveloped. These areas contain less tissue, are smaller in size than normal and therefore do not feel the same sense of inhibition and normal empathetic response of fully developed brains. They don't perceive their victims as

Introduction

anything more than objects or experience the same fear of getting caught as would others.

In terms of notoriety, the most infamous serial killers of all time are men. One of the earliest recorded was Gilles de Rais, a French Nobleman from the 15th century. Intensely interested in the occult, by the age of 28, he began luring young boys to his estate where he raped and killed them. The 19th century belonged to Jack the Ripper, who murdered five prostitutes in the streets of London in 1888. In the more modern era, there are Jeffrey Dahmer, who lured teenage boys to his home, where he drugged them, killed them, raped them and ate their remains, and Anatoly Onoprienko (aka Citizen 0), who confessed to killing no less than 52 people in the Ukraine, including whole families— followed directives from God.

Women as Serial Killers

Throughout history, women are significantly in the minority when it comes to serial killers. Of those who do qualify, more than 85% lived in the United States.

Unlike their male counterparts, women serial killers tend to act out of easily identifiable motives, overall- revenge, greed and mental illness. Similar to men, women fall into two categories: those that act alone and those that work with partners. Regardless of category, women seldom evidence the kind of sexual depravity and premeditated torture attributed to men, or exhibits the same degree of obsessive and controlling behavior.

Women who act alone are most often "mature, careful, deliberate, socially adept, and highly organized. They usually attack victims in their home or place of work."[1] The three most popular methods of disposal are poison, stabbing and suffocation, with shooting a close runner-up. The three most common classifications are those of the Black Widow—kill multiple spouses, lovers or other family members; Angels of Death and Baby Farmers—who kill under the pretense of providing health care; and those that kill for profit.

Women, who act in partnership, tend to be younger, more aggressive, vicious, and more spontaneous, relying upon weapons of convenience, such as knives and axes. Greed and acceptance are the most common motivators.

The first recorded woman serial killer in the United States was Livinia Fisher. She was born in 1792. She and her husband owned and operated a hotel in South Carolina. She would poison her male guests and her husband would later come along and make sure they died. They would then steal their valuables and do away with the bodies. In the course of time they were eventually caught and hanged. Livinia was 28 at the time.

Perhaps the most despicable woman serial killer in US history was Dorothea Puente. After a number of failed marriages, Puente started dating older men. She would steal and cash their benefit checks. After doing a stretch in prison, in 1980, she opened her own boarding house and catered to the elderly, from whom she would manipulate the better part of their social security checks. Many of her older male tenants went missing or died suddenly and without obvious cause.

In the fall of '85, Puente paid a handyman to dispose of a luggage trunk, which he did leaving it in a wooded area beside a river. A local fisherman observed the trunk and informed the police. Authorities found the remains of an old man stuffed inside the trunk. The follow-up investigation uncovered the remains of multiple bodies buried out behind the boarding house. Despite Puente's claim they had all died of natural causes, a jury convicted and imprisoned her for life. She died in 2011 at the age of 82.

Women Serial Killers in 19th Century New York

The women who serve as the subjects for this book all share compelling stories, and in the case of a few, the actions could be considered within reason given their circumstances. Most are from north-central New York along the Erie Canal and associated water ways, which is consistent with the rural nature of the state at that time and the limited means of travel. The others lived in Manhattan or within close proximity. These were the baby killers.

A majority of these women were dubbed Black Widow killers. Polly Frisch murdered as a result of her twisted sense of love. Elizabeth McCraney, Francis Shrouder, Angenette Haight and Mary Runkle found their motivation in greed. Caroline D. Sorgenfrie seemed both greedy and mentally disturbed. Lizzie Halliday suffered without doubt from mental illness. Elizabeth Van Valkenburgh perhaps bore the pain of spousal abuse; but this I will leave to the reader.

In addition, there are four baby farmers, a title given to women accused of murdering infants for profit. Two, Margaret McCloskey and Rozilla Worcester lived in Manhattan. A third, Catherine Claus resided in Maspeth, Queens. The

Introduction

fourth, Cynthia McDonald, came from upstate Rochester.

Mrs. Phebe Westlake occupied a class of her own, both a Black Widow and an Angel of Death.

Included also are two teen-aged girls, 14 year-old Ella Holdridge and 13 year-old Fanny Scofield. Combined, they caused the deaths of no less than seven children under the age of seven.

Finally, there are the stories of Roxanna Druse and Mary Antone. Although neither formally earned the title of serial killer, their murderess activity earned each a place of distinction in the State's history as it pertains to executions.

To properly frame the stories within a historical context of the communities in New York State in which the crimes and trials occurred, each tale is preceded by a summary sketch of the origins and development of the counties where the murders took place, and where appropriate, specific towns. I also thought it fit, as a means of emphasizing the stark depravity of these infamous citizens, to provide for events and notable persons whose contributions to the area were invaluable to its history.

To those they care for

"Be afraid…Be very afraid"

BLACK WIDOWS

Chapter 1

Lizzie Halliday

The story of Lizzie Halliday takes place in the territory stretching throughout Sullivan and Orange County, and includes the towns of Newburgh (Orange County), Burlingham, Walden and Monticello in Sullivan County. For those less familiar, Newburgh is located just off the west banks of the Hudson River, about 60 miles directly north of New York City. The town of Burlingham is approximately 8 miles west north-west of Newburgh and north of Middletown. The village of Walden is on the road between Newburgh and Burlingham. The city of Monticello is 15 miles due west.

In 1894 many viewed Sullivan County, as holding "a reputation for quiet and sturdy morality, inhabited almost entirely by the farming class" and counted on for "quiet monotony [as] its distinguishing feature."[1]

The lands around the current City of Newburgh were first explored by the Europeans who followed after Henry Hudson, early in the 17th century. It wasn't one hundred years later that the new arrivals from Germany settled there, with the English and Scots to follow. In 1783, during the Revolutionary War, a small group of military officers conspired to overthrow the fledgling United States Government, but were dissuaded by George Washington.

In 1763, a legislative decree established the Precinct of Newburgh. It formally became a township in 1788, a village in 1800, and finally a city in 1865. Farms and various mills made up the primary settlements that used local water sources for power. Throughout the latter part of the 19th century, the town produced gun powder and masonry bricks, as the land yielded an abundant amount of the resources to produce these products. The Precinct even produced a large share of the bricks used in the construction of New York City. Newburgh also holds the distinction of being the first fully electrified city in America.

Today, Newburgh is known more as an upper-middle class city, attracting families that value a rural sense of life but requiring a proximity to the jobs and amenities of a metropolitan area.

Walden, settled around 1650, attracted Europeans to the fertile lands along the banks of the Wallkill and Paltz Rivers, once inhabited by Native Americans. Most of these early settlers earned their livings as farmers, craftsmen and traders. In the beginning of the 19th century citizens harnessed the power of the rivers and falls to provide for industry. By the middle of the century, Walden became a major producer of cotton and wool fabrics and officially incorporated as a village in 1855.

By the turn of the 20th century, Walden saw an increase in the number of single family homes and established dominance throughout the area in manufacturing, commerce and banking. However, that all began to change in the 1950s. Throughout the next 30-40 years many local companies lost business to competing markets further down south. Today, Walden is best known for its banking services and continues to thrive as an attractive area for families.

Burlingham is located in the Shawangunk Ridge. The ridge is the eastern-most extent of the Appalachian Mountains and spreads from north of New Paltz south-west through the counties of Ulster, Sullivan and Orange and down into Pennsylvania and New Jersey. The ridge is covered by dense trees and sprinkled with wetlands, bogs, waterfalls and ice caves which tend to stay frozen even during the summer months. The naturally occurring lakes and ponds in the area contain water that is extremely acidic due to the lack of buffering characteristics found in most rock formations.

Today, much of the area is contained by public lands and preserves and is available to the public for recreational activity such as hiking.

Politics & Prose

Geraldine Ferraro became the first female candidate for vice president representing a major party. Born in Newburgh, New York in 1935, she attended

Lizzy Halliday

Mount Saint Mary's Parochial School. However, her father died when she was just nine and her mother squandered what money they had on poor investments. As a result, the family begrudgingly moved to the Bronx. Geraldine chose to attend school in Tarrytown at the Marymount Academy, which her mother paid for with rental income from property owned in Italy.

In 1956, Ferraro graduated from Manhattan Marymount College and took a job as an elementary school teacher. Not satisfied with teaching, she soon enrolled in law school, graduating with a degree from Fordham University in 1960. She was admitted to the bar one year later.

Initially, she worked as a real estate lawyer, but soon became involved with the Democratic Party in the early 70s. She took her first politically-connected position in 1974 when Queens County appointed her as an Assistant District Attorney. Frustrated with her level of pay as compared to her male colleagues, the then Secretary of New York State, Mario Cuomo, suggested she run for Congress. She did so in 1978 and won.

Due to her success in Washington, in 1984 Walter Mondale chose her as his running mate. The selection of a female as a candidate for vice presidency met with considerable resistance and many attempted to discredit her politically and personally. Ronald Reagan won the election by a landslide.

Following her failed run at the Whitehouse, Ferraro went on to have a distinguished career serving as a Senator and as an Ambassador. She passed away in March of 2011 after an extended illness.

James Patterson

James B. Patterson, the author best known for his series based on the exploits of the fictional psychologist Alex Cross, was born in Newburgh in 1947. He attended both Manhattan College and Vanderbilt University where he majored in English.

Prior to devoting his time solely to his pursuits as a novelist, Patterson worked in advertising from which he retired from in 1996. He published his first Alex Cross novel in 1976, called *The Thomas Berryman Number*. He has since written 95 others, 19 of which have spent time as the #1 best seller on the *New York Times* sales list. The Cross novels form the most popular detective series in the last 10 years. The sales of these books and his other endeavors have provided Patterson with a net worth of more the $300 million. Patterson acknowledges that he often uses ghostwriters to produce his books, stating that he is better at coming up with plot ideas than actually telling the story.

Which begs the question: What would Alex Cross think of Lizzie Halliday?

The Worst Woman on Earth

Lizzie Halliday, born Elizabeth McNally in Ireland in 1861, with her family came to the United States in the late 1880s. Once in America, the McNally's settled in Pennsylvania where Elizabeth, at the time in her early twenties, married a man by the name of "Ketspool" Brown, aka Charles Hopkins. They had one son together. Charles died soon after which authorities determined to be due to "natural causes". After this Elizabeth committed her son to a state institution for the "feeble minded".

Over the next few years, Elizabeth married four more times. Her second husband, Artemas Brewster, described as a broke-down veteran from Greenwich Village in Washington County, died within their first year together. Acquaintances knew he endured Elizabeth's constant beatings and hair pulling.[2] Her third husband, George Smith was an army comrade of Mr. Brewster. Despite witnessing the torment Brewster went through at the hands of his wife, Smith married Elizabeth, anyway. She promptly attempted to kill him by poisoning his tea. While Smith recovered under the care of a physician, Elizabeth ran off with a man many years her senior named Hiram Parkinson. It is debatable as to if they actually married, but regardless they later parted company.

Elizabeth, now calling herself Lizzie, traveled to Vermont where she wasted little time in marrying the only one of her spouses who's age fell close to her own, a Charles Pleysteil. The marriage lasted only two weeks, after which, for reasons unknown, Elizabeth again picked up and left the state. There is no reason to believe Mr. Pleysteil suffered any misfortune. After leaving Charles, there is some record of her formalizing a relationship with a man known only as Henry; a justice of the peace presided over the nuptials.[3]

Lizzie, accompanied by her son, now released from the confinement of the institution where she left him, surfaced again in 1888 in Newburgh calling at the home of a childhood friend, Margaret McQuinlan. McQuinlan's

Lizzy Halliday

family lived alongside the McNally's while they all still resided in Ireland and both families came to the States at the same time. She and her husband, John McQuinlan, owned a house at 1213 North Street. It is known that they had at least one child, a daughter by the name of Sarah. John McQuinlan owned and operated a local saloon. Lizzie and her son became welcomed as guests and may have boarded at the home for a short while.

Lizzie soon returned to Philadelphia where she rented an apartment with a small store front at 2480 Kensington Avenue. Then, during the blizzard of '88, she set it on fire in an attempt to collect on the insurance policy. The fire destroyed not only her store, but also the buildings on either side. Arrested and charged with both fraud and arson, Lizzie served two years in Eastern State Penitentiary.

In 1891, following her release, she moved to Sullivan County, where she married a man in his seventies by the name of Paul Halliday. He had two known sons by a previous wife. The first, Paul Halliday, Jr., was married to a woman by the name of Addie. They lived locally. Many believed the second boy, John, to be developmentally handicapped. Together they lived as a family in nearby Burlingham. Shortly after, the residence, described as a cabin, went up in flames burning John to death. Police, however, did not suspect arson.

The surviving couple then moved into another house, and in 1893, the unsuspecting Mr. Halliday suddenly disappeared without a trace. The authorities, by now sufficiently suspicious, searched the house. A local constable by the name of Scott noted a section of carpet and a cut of rope, both stained with blood, and found a bullet beneath the bed.

The search then moved to the barn behind the home. The floor was dug up and two bodies discovered, neither of which proved to be Mr. Halliday. Instead, discoverers found the deceased persons of Margaret McQuinlan and her daughter, Sarah, who had recently gone missing sometime between August 30th and September 2nd. Certain they occupied right trail, authorities continued to search the property. Subsequently searchers located Mr. Halliday's body beneath the house. The assailant shot Mr. Halliday at least two times and mutilated the corpse. Examiners found the killer also shot Sarah three times in the heart. Police later found a loaded revolver and two boxes of cartridges in a closet in the house.

Detectives arrested and charged Lizzie Halliday with the murder of all three victims and suspected she killed a fourth person, a local peddler, by the name of Samuel Hutch. Authorities found Hutch murdered in 1890, the body being recovered from the old lead mines within 10 miles of the Halliday home. The local people in Walker Valley vowed to hang her on the spot.

The Trial

Lizzie awaited trial for more than a year while incarcerated in Monticello. During this time, she did the best she could to present herself as crazy, ranting, raving and refusing to keep herself clean; her hair grew matted and disheveled. Twice she tried to take her own life, once by cutting her own throat with a piece of metal she fashioned from the heel of her shoe, and the second, by attempting to hang herself with a piece of rope she managed to obtain. After that, the tending sheriff, Harrison Beecher, secured her to the floor with a chain. Lizzie responded by refusing to eat in an attempt to starve herself to death. Her detainers force fed her against her will.

Judge Edwards presided over the trial, which started on June 18, 1894. Lizzie professed her innocence in the deaths of her husband and the two McQuinlan ladies. She blamed the murders on a band of gypsy-like brigands whom she alleged operated throughout the mountains and valley. She claimed they would waylay unsuspecting peddlers and desolate women, stealing their wares and valuables, and in the end murder them and dispose of their bodies in the old lead mine. Instead of convincing the court of her innocence, her knowledge of particular details led the court to propose that Lizzie married Paul Halliday to serve as "a decoy for [the] band that did the murders."[4]

Ultimately, the trial revealed that Lizzie lured the McQuinlans, one by one from their home under the pretense of helping her with cleaning a large boarding house in Walden for $2. Mrs. Evaline S. Wright, a neighbor of the McQuinlans, attested to this fact. She identified Lizzie as the woman who called herself Smith and came with a buckboard wagon and a horse to collect Mrs. McQuinlan on a Wednesday in August.

Mr. McQuinlan, in his testimony to follow, informed the court that Lizzie showed up at his house three nights later on a Saturday. She told him that his wife had fallen and became seriously injured. When he said he would immediately come and fetch her, Lizzie told him the doctor wouldn't allow it, and instead, to send Sarah to attend to her mother until she recovered.

Lizzy Halliday

There in the court room, attorneys showed Mr. Quinlan property they believed to belong to his daughter. He positively identified her dress, cloak, watch, ring and hat.[5] Police found two additional rings, both belonging to Mrs. McQuinlan, in Lizzie's closet after the discovery of the bodies.

On June 27th, the jury found Lizzie guilty of the murders and sentenced her to hang. On the way out of the court room, she attacked the accompanying sheriff, Harrison Beecher, biting his hand through the gloves he wore. He developed a serious infection as the result of the bite. In two different versions of the story, the resultant wound became so badly infected that he either needed to have the hand amputated,[6] or he contracted a fatal poisoning of the blood. In both reports, he died.[7]

Matteawan Prison for the Criminally Insane

Governor Flowers granted Lizzie clemency after the judge originally sentenced her to execution in the electric chair based on being found insane by a group of physicians. Instead, he changed her sentence to incarceration for life in the Matteawan Prison for the Criminally Insane.

While there she continued to exhibit dangerous tendencies and other inmates and the attendants generally gave her a wide berth. In 1897, she took offense at her treatment by one of the attendants. Together with a second inmate, Jane Shannon—considered the most dangerous inmate in the institution, they isolated the attendant in a bathroom. Shannon knocked the attendant, Miss Kate Ward, to the ground and jumped on her. Halliday then stuffed a towel into her mouth, and the two of them began to pound the victim with their fists, Lizzie pulled out Ward's hair and scratched her face mercilessly with her finger nails. When rescued from the assault, Miss Ward's liberators found her unconscious. She did, however, manage to survive with no lingering injuries. Doctors secured both attackers in isolation.

Six years later, after relatively stable behavior, Lizzie struck again, only this time more viciously, murdering a prison nurse named Miss Nellie Wicks. Only 24 years old, Wicks showed Lizzie more kindness than any other person. According to the details, hospital directors promoted Miss Wicks to the head of the women's unit, due to her ability to relate with the inmates. In her new position, she developed a fondness for the difficult to manage Lizzie and gave her certain privileges within the group. Lizzie, in turn, reciprocated the kindness and appeared to develop a sort of maternal affection for Miss Wicks.

After a time, Miss Wicks informed the group, including Lizzie, that she would soon be leaving the institution to pursue her studies to become a medical nurse. Lizzie begged her not to leave. Nevertheless, Miss Wicks remained resolute. Over her last few days, Lizzie made verbal threats, saying that she would kill the young nurse rather than see her leave. As Lizzie often made threats of this sort, those around her ignored her ultimatums.

On her final day in the institution, at 8:00 in the morning, Miss Wicks entered a bathroom. Lizzie slipped in behind her and knocked her to the floor. Before the nurse could react, Lizzie took her keys and locked the door from the inside. She then returned to the defenseless young woman and, using a pair of scissors she was allowed for sewing, proceeded to stab Miss Wicks over two hundred times in the face and head. Her screams alerted the other attendants who eventually managed to come to her aid. It was too late. She died less than an hour later.

While being taken to a cell in solitary confinement, Lizzie said, rather calmly, "She won't leave me now."[8]

Interestingly enough, an article entitled "Lizzie Halliday Getting Better" appeared in the *Middletown Daily Argus* following her first year in Matteawan. The article stated that the insane murderess "lost the fierce look that characterized her insanity and in its place has come the light of returning reason."[9]

The Death and Legend of Lizzie Halliday

While incarcerated, the legend of Lizzie Halliday continued to grow.

In an article that appeared in the *Alexandria Gazette*[10], Halliday, whom many already called the "Wolf Woman of Sullivan County", was given the additional title of "Gipsy Queen". The piece claimed she lead a "little band which roved over the Hudson and Mohawk Valleys."

The article goes on to say, inaccurately, that she and the band came to Burlingham in 1902, where Paul Halliday fell in love with the Gipsy Queen. Following their marriage, the band of gypsies "celebrated the event, elected another queen and moved on."

Lizzy Halliday

To further add intrigue and mystery to the murders of Mr. Halliday and the McQuinlans, the article attributes their deaths to ritual shootings described as "… shot five times in the heart, the five bullets forming a circle."

On June 28, 1918, while still incarcerated in the Matteawan Asylum, Lizzie Halliday, once described as the "worst woman on earth,"[11] passed away. She was 58 years of age.

Victims-8

Chapter 2

Elizabeth P. McCraney

Oneonta, known as "the City of Hills", gets its name from the Native American word *o-neny-onda*, which, loosely translated, means "rock sticking out". A prominent characteristic of the city is the exposed bedrock of its surrounding hills, known as Table rocks. It is located in southern Otsego County, approximately 170 miles north, north-west of New York City.

In its earliest history, Iroquois and Algonquin Indians inhabited the lands. However, the Algonquin proved to be the more dominant people and drove out the Iroquois tribes.

The first Europeans, primarily German and Dutch farmers, arrived in 1775 and settled in the Susquehanna Valley and the Oneonta Plains along Otego Creek. Around 1800 they formed the first hamlet and named it Milfordville.

In the mid-1860s, the Delaware and Hudson Railroad expanded into Oneonta and as part of that expansion, the company financed the construction of the largest roundhouse in the world at the time. Engineers only designed early steam locomotives to move forward. The roundhouse used a turntable to swing the locomotives around and return them to their point of origin. As a result of this structure, the town of Oneonta experienced significant growth and began to establish itself as a center for industry in the northern part of the state. In 1993, crews demolished the roundhouse.

Today, Oneonta is primarily recognized as a college town. Home of both Oneonta State College and Hartwick College, during the school year the population of the city more than doubles.

Elizabeth P. McCraney

Authors and Lawyers

James Fennimore Cooper, author of *The Last of the Mohicans*, was born in Burlington, New Jersey, but spent the majority of his life in Cooperstown, New York. In 1833 he returned from living abroad in Europe and a year later, after 16 years away, decided to reopen his ancestral mansion, known as Otsego Hall, in Cooperstown. He lived there until his death in 1851.

William Henry Bissell was born in Hartwick in 1811. He moved to Illinois in 1837 where he became a member of the House of Representatives. He was elected the 11ᵗʰ governor of the state in 1857 and served in that position until his death in 1860.

Levi S. Chatfield was an American lawyer and politician born in the Town of Morris in 1808. He held the positions of both a member of the New York State Assembly and its Speaker from 1838 to 1842. In 1847, he ran for Attorney General as a democrat but lost to Ambrose L. Jordan, a Whig. He ran again in 1849 and won, and then won again in 1851. He resigned in 1853. In 1859, he and L. L. Bundy teamed together to defend Elizabeth P. McCraney against the charge of murder.

And that brings us to our story:

Early History

Elizabeth P. McCraney was born in Warren, Ohio, but spent a significant part of her early adult life in Otsego, New York. Although the details are somewhat sketchy, she married twice while residing in the state. She married first, sometime around 1840, to Abram Clark, an Otsego County native. She had at least one child with him and perhaps a second. Eventually they divorced. Mr. Clark died shortly after due to unknown causes. Local resources list the death of at least one child.

Elizabeth then married her second husband, also from Otsego, Spencer Baker. They too had at least one child, a daughter Lucia, and possibly a second. Either way, Spencer Baker, too, died unexpectedly, as did his brother, Allen, and Allen's wife, all in succession and over a short period of time. They all resided in the same home. The *Jamesville Daily Gazette of Wisconsin*, almost

30 years later, referred to the death of a second child, but it is uncertain as to if that child came from Elizabeth's marriage to Mr. Baker or to Mr. Clark. Regardless, no one found reason at the time to suspect any involvement on Elizabeth's part.

Following the death of Mr. Baker, Elizabeth moved to Wisconsin with their daughter, Lucia. Her father had come to the area 40 years prior and established himself as a preacher of some reputation. She also had a sister living there with whom she went to live. Her brother-in-law, Thomas Burnett, their daughter and two other unidentified persons also lived in the residence. In 1849, all five died from arsenic poisoning. Authorities arrested and tried Elizabeth, but could not convict her.

In 1857 Elizabeth, using the name Mrs. Spencer Baker, and Lucia returned to Oneonta, taking up residence at the Oneonta House. After inheriting her father's estate, which included an expansive farm along the east banks of the Mississippi in southern Wisconsin, Elizabeth became financially well off. Her finery and plumed hats, rare commodities in the placid and small country town—isolated from the rest of the world by scarce transportation and limited forms of communication—soon became a source of much envy among the local ladies. The scandal surrounding Elizabeth only heightened when it became known that she attracted the eye of a well-respected local gentleman by the name of John McCraney.

Mr. McCraney was a widower with two daughters of his own, Huldah and Sarah. He and Elizabeth fell in love. In February of 1859, and after the appropriate courting, they married. Following their marriage, Elizabeth convinced John to take a vacation from Oneonta, which they did in July of that year. They left the children with neighbors and returned to Wisconsin. While there, Elizabeth sold the farm, and the two newlyweds took some time to tour the west. They returned to Oneonta in October and took up permanent residence on Dietz Street.

Both of the older daughters attended Oneonta High School. Huldah, due to her popularity and pretty face, looked forward to being crowned the May Queen, when on May 1st she fell ill. According to his recollections, Willard V. Huntington, in his book *Oneonta Memories*, wrote:

Huldah Ann McCraney had made her usual preparations for attending church and passing her

father's house sat down on the front steps, being
suddenly taken ill and unable to proceed. She was
assisted into the house and went to be, never in her
mortal frame to arise again.[1]

The family summoned local physician, Dr. Samuel H. Case, to the
house. His initial diagnosis showed a basic malady and he advised Huldah
to remain in bed. However, the next day she felt no better and over the next
couple of days she complained of aches and pains throughout her body and
an abnormal thirst.

Dr. Case made a number of subsequent visits to the house, and although
he commented as to the strangeness of the case, he made no other diagnosis.
The neighbors, however, particularly Mrs. S. J. Cook and Mrs. Jacob S. Dietz,
expressed their concerns privately. Both became familiar with Elizabeth's
reputation and the rumors associated with her past. Others took to covering
their wells at night, afraid that their infamous neighbor might have greater and
more evil designs.

On May 11th, ten days after first feeling ill, Huldah died. Mrs. Dietz, who
had been taking turns caring for her during her illness, noticed peculiar spots
or lesions on Huldah's lips. She immediately brought her suspicions to the
attention of the coroner, a Mr. Bartlett, but he initially dismissed them. After
others expressed similar concerns, however, he ordered a formal investigation.

They exhumed the body on May 18th, five days after burial. The coroner
removed a number of organs and sawed off the skull to remove the brain.
This postmortem examination performed by Dr. J. S. Sprague and Dr. Horace
Lathrop Jr., both of the Albany Medical College; with the assistance of Dr.
C. Porter, also of the same institution determined the presence of significant
traces of arsenic.

The Trial

The Coroner's Inquiry, held in Otsego County, commenced on or about June 10th
of that year. Apparently, Elizabeth testified in her own defense and presented
herself as cold and calculated. Witnesses described her physically as having

a "dashing appearance [and] a remarkable degree of beauty" which had only diminished slightly with age. She was fifty at the time. Intellectually, many assumed her to have 'great decision of character and uncommon executive ability".[2] Ultimately, prosecutors accused her of administering daily doses of arsenic to Huldah while pretending to nurse her.

On the 23rd of that month, after considerable deliberation, the coroner's jury found Elizabeth P. McCraney guilty of *willfully and feloniously* bringing about the death of her step-daughter. The court formally charged, arrested and remanded her before the Grand Jury in Cooperstown.

Fearing for her safety, the local authorities secreted Elizabeth out of Oneonta and to Cooperstown in a horse-drawn carriage along the road at night. Nevertheless, a prearranged signal by local boys, followed by gun shots and the ringing of the church bell, alerted the neighbors. They raced out ahead of the carriage and placed physical obstacles in their path over the Oneonta creek bridge. One of the authorities, Willis Snow, tried in vain to clear the way. Instead, the party turned from the road and exited the town over a second bridge off of Main Street.[3]

McCraney's trial started on December 10th in the Court of Oyer and Terminer. Elizabeth entered a plea of not guilty. District Attorney E. Countryman argued the State's case. Levi S. Chatfield of Laurens and L. L. Bundy of Oneonta represented Elizabeth.[4] Hundreds of townspeople attended the trials proceedings.

A review of the sworn and written statements of Dr. Case, Dr. Sprague and Dr. Lathrop revealed none of the learned doctors, following the postmortem of the step-daughter, found evidence which "would account satisfactorily for death" other than the presence of arsenic.[5] Dr. Porter, who conducted the chemical analysis, further tested a syringe found in the girl's room. The results confirmed it to be tainted with arsenic. Prosecutors believed that the syringe was used to inject the poison via the rectum. In addition, evidence showed that Elizabeth had recently purchased the poison from a local apothecary.

On the part of her defense, L. L. Bundy asserted the doctors' reports noted only trace amounts of arsenic in Huldah's organs and further made the claim that Dr. Porter came about his position at the Albany Medical School not based on merit but by "favoritism", thereby questioning his expertise. He also suggested the green color of the bed sheets upon which Huldah slept contained arsenic and the poison found in her body resulted from the green dye.[6]

Elizabeth P. McCraney

On the 15th of December, Attorney General Myers summed up the trial for the people of the jury. One day later, the jury returned with a verdict of not guilty.

Following her acquittal, Elizabeth returned to Oneonta and continued to live in the house on Dietz Street with her husband, John McCraney, and their two children. Locals, however, continuously harassed her, especially the younger folk, who threw rocks at her windows and heavy objects onto her roof. Many people burned her in effigy and some of the more influential citizens held a rally at Military Hall on Main Street demanding she leave the village.

Eventually, the commotion surrounding Elizabeth gained national attention and brought front and center the death of her second husband's brother, Allen Baker. On January 9, 1861, two years after her first trial, authorities exhumed the remains of Mr. Baker from his place of rest in Edison's Corners and sent them to Dr. Porter for chemical analysis. Test results proved that he too died from arsenic poisoning.

Police arrested Elizabeth again and charged with the murder of her then brother-in-law. This trial started on June 20 and took place in the same court room as the first. Five days later, after deliberating for 48 hours, the jury again found her not guilty for lack of evidence.

Once more, Elizabeth P. McCraney returned to Oneonta, where she remained married to John, who professed her innocence until the end. He died on September 16, 1865. After that date, there is no further information on Mrs. McCraney, other than a line in the *Oneonta Star*, August 2, 1913, which stated, "Mrs. McCraney survived him for a long time afterward."[7] It is possible she moved to Nebraska where she passed away.[8] She may or may not have been buried alongside her daughter Lucia in the McCraney family plot on the shore of the Susquehanna River. As for her motive, that too she took to the grave.

Victims-9

Chapter 3

Elizabeth Van Valkenburgh

The city of Fulton, named after Robert Fulton, the inventor of the steamboat, is located in Oswego County in western New York not too far from the shore of Lake Ontario. It covers an area of less than five square miles, and is divided by the Oswego River. In 1835 officials formally recognized the section of the city west of the river, known as Oswego Falls, and considered it a separate village from that of the Village of Fulton. In 1906, the two merged and became an incorporated city. There are two bridges now joining the two sides.

In the early 20th century, the textile industry became the city's primary trade and hosted the American Woolen Mills which produced many of the uniforms worn by American troops in both World Wars. In 1903, Fulton also became home of the first chocolate manufacturing facility in the United States when Peter Kohler, founder of the Nestle brand, came here to launch his business.

Johnstown, New York, is around 120 miles due east from Fulton. It is located between Little Falls and Amsterdam, and is at present the government seat of Fulton County—not to be confused with Fulton in Oswego County.

Sir William Johnson founded Johnstown in 1762. Johnson, originally from Ireland, came to America in 1732. He made his living as a trader and without delay learned the languages of the various Native American tribes inhabiting the region. He later served on the side of the British during the French and Indian War and rose to the rank of Major General. His influence with the Native Americans, and in particular the Iroquois, became essential in obtaining their cooperation against the French. As recognition of his invaluable service, following the war, the Mohawk of Canajoharie granted Johnson land, more than 80,000 acres, that later became Johnstown, which he named after his son.

Although William Johnson died prior to the Revolutionary War, his lands served as one of the last places of refuge for British troops and loyalists against the Continental troops. On October 25, 1781, the Revolutionaries led by Colonel Marinus Willett of Johnstown, drove the final remnants of those loyal to England from the area. At the turn of the century, 1803, officials incorporated Johnstown as a village. In 1895, they incorporated the City of Johnstown.

Cambridge is almost 60 miles due east from Johnstown and no more than five miles from the border of Vermont. At the time of our story, and still largely today, it is a decidedly a rural community, characterized by dense swathes of woods and open farm land. The state formally recognized the area as a village in the late 18th century.

Early Years

Albert Lindley Lee, best known for his exploits in the Civil War, was born in Fulton, New York in 1834. He went on to attend Union College in Schenectady where he studied Law. He graduated in 1853. He started his Law practice in New York City, but soon after moved to Kansas where he became involved in the newspaper business. During his time serving as a justice of the Kansas Supreme Court the Civil War broke out.

Lee joined the Union Army as a major in the 7th Kansas Calvary where he served with bravery in more than 8 major campaigns, including the battle of Corinth and the assault on Vicksburg. The Army elevated him to the rank of brigadier general and they twice required him to take command of two different battle fields. During the second of these commands he received a wound to the head, but he recovered and fought two more battles. In Louisiana, at his last battle, his troops routed the remains of a weak Confederate resistance.

Following the war, Lee became an editor for a newspaper in New Orleans. In the later part of his career, he returned to New York City where he became involved in business, and above all banking. He died in 1907.

Daniel Cady, the father of Fulton County, was born in Canaan in 1773, which is approximately 15 miles south-east of Albany. He first took up the trade of shoemaker but suffered an injury which cost him vision in one eye. He then took up the study of law and was admitted to the bar in 1795.

His intelligence and talent aside, Cady's greatest influence derived from his marriage to Margaret Livingston, whom he married after moving to Johnstown in 1799. Margaret was related to Robert Fulton and by marriage to the Jacob Astor fortune. Cady used these connections to grow his own business interests, build his own personal fortune and become one of the largest landowners in the region.

From 1806 to 1814, Cady served as a member of the legislature. In 1816, he returned to Johnstown to practice law. In 1847 voters elected him onto the New York Supreme Court. He served until 1855. He died in Johnstown in 1859 and is buried there.

Infamous

All which is known about Elizabeth Van Valkenburgh's earlier life comes from her own signed confession. She was born in Bennington, Vermont in 1799. At just the age of five her parents died and she went to live across the border in Cambridge, New York. She had neither an education nor any degree of religious upbringing.

At the age of 20, she married her first husband. They relocated to Pennsylvania where they had four children. Many described the town as rural with the nearest church being more than 14 miles away. Six years later, the family moved to Johnstown, New York.

In 1833, upset by the amount of time he spent drinking in the local tavern, owned by a Mr. Terrill, Elizabeth poisoned her husband's rum with arsenic. He didn't die right then and there but the poison left him unwell. His symptoms worsened each day. He managed to go about business as usual for a period of time, including going to work, before his organs shut down and he died. Doctors attributed his death to dyspepsia—an abnormal functioning of the stomach and small intestine—and exposure to the elements.

In 1834, not long after her first husband passed, Elizabeth married John

Elizabeth Van Valkenburgh

Van Valkenburgh. Together they produced two additional children. Elizabeth described her marriage as an unhappy one. She claimed her husband was "addicted to liquor; misused the children when under its influence, and at such times...," she added, "... we frequently quarreled."[1]

Ten years later, in 1844, the disharmony in the household reached the point where Elizabeth's two oldest sons offered to buy her a home of her own and provide for the upkeep of her and the younger children. This suggestion angered John, and he refused to allow Elizabeth to leave. That's when she first thought to do away with him as she did her first husband.

In the spring, somewhere around late April, she had the occasion to be away from home, visiting friends by the name of Mrs. Zeiley and Mrs. Mitchell, the latter of which had a son. Annoyed with the number of rats infesting her home and seeking a means by which to be rid of them, Elizabeth asked the Mitchell boy to procure some arsenic for her, which he did.

Around the same time, Elizabeth's husband absconded on an alcohol fueled rampage and left their home for a period of eight days. Upon his return, he continued to imbibe to excess and did nothing to provide for the needs of the home or the children.

Elizabeth became so despondent, that she reacted by poisoning his tea with the unused portion of the arsenic she obtained to exterminate the rats. Although he became ill, the dose was insufficient to kill him. They summoned a local physician, Doctor Burdick. The doctor treated John and though he would never again be well, he did manage to recover some of his strength.

During this time of convalescence, John most furiously objected to the notion of Elizabeth moving out on her own. Seeing no way out of her abusive situation and afraid he would continue to live, she again arranged for the Mitchell boy to provide her with more arsenic.

This time she resolved to kill her husband; Elizabeth placed the arsenic in the bottom of a tea cup and added boiling water to ensure it would dissolve. Next she added the brandy. With the poison then undetectable, she served the concoction to John. The brandy contained such an elevated dose, right away he began vomiting and convulsing and continued to do so until he passed out.

Elizabeth remained in the household with the dying John, expecting his death at any minute. He, however, was stubborn and hung on. As the days passed, his condition became general knowledge and many suspected he may have been poisoned.

The following Saturday or Sunday, and with her husband still alive, if only just, Elizabeth became aware that she would be arrested for her deed. That night she fled to the home of Mrs. Wakefield, an acquaintance living in Kingsboro. The authorities discovered her there the following day, arrested her and took her back to Fulton. That night, she again fled but this time to the barn of a neighbor by the name of McClaren. Attempting to hide herself in the hayloft, she fell and broke her leg. Police again took her into custody, but this time, not taking any further chances, they put her in a cell in the county jail in Fulton. Her husband died on Tuesday.

Trial and Execution

In his summation of the trial, the presiding judge emphasized the fairness of the proceedings. He complimented the jury, which he reminded Elizabeth was of her own choosing, and the efforts of her attorney to defend her. He also expressed that she had been given every benefit of doubt due to the claims of her husband's alleged abusiveness towards both her and the children.[2] He then declared her guilty.

Prior to announcing the sentence, he reminded her that he only acted upon his duty, and for no other reason, and the life of a murderer is forfeit so with hope others may think twice before doing the same. He then admonished her for depriving her husband of the foreknowledge of her attack which left him unable to defend himself. He called the crime revolting. Further, as if he ignored John's abusive nature and general failure as a husband, he stated the act was made even more despicable given she promised to love, to cherish and to obey and that she, by her actions, deprived the children of their father.[3] He then sentenced her to hang by the neck until dead.

In response to the appeal of her death sentence, which had been supported by ten of the jurors who tried the case, the Governor of New York, Silas Wright, provided a brief statement to the court which in part read:

> **Her age, her state of health, her poverty, her young family, and more than all, her sex, has appealed to my feelings with fearful force in her favor; but her**

Elizabeth Van Valkenburgh

awful crime ... [has] forbid that I should yield to those feelings[4]

On January 24, 1846, two days after providing a signed statement acknowledging her guilt, including having poisoned her first husband, assistants carried Elizabeth Van Valkenburgh, confined to a rocking chair due to her broken leg (and rather excessive weight), to the gallows. Prior to having the noose placed about her neck, she asked to speak and the executioner granted her permission. She took the opportunity to warn others against the evil of alcohol. According to witnesses, Valkenburgh, rocked gently back and forth in her chair when the trap door beneath her suddenly opened and fulfilled its task in gruesome fashion.

Victims-3

Chapter 4

Angenette B.S. Haight

DeRuyter, New York is a rural town located in central New York, approximately 20 miles northeast of Cortland and 30 miles south of Syracuse. The Dutch originally settled the area, originally part of Whitestone, in the later part of the 18th century and many referred to it as Tromp Township, named after Admiral Marten von Tromp of Holland. Officials renamed the township in 1798 after another Dutch admiral, Michiel DeRuyter. They incorporated it as a village in 1833 at which time its population was little more than 700.

The village itself is located in a valley surrounded by four hills through which runs the Tioughnioga River. Rich soil and an abundant supply of fresh water attracted the original settlers. Serving as a midway point between the surrounding and more established settlements, the town's first enterprises were taverns, inns and stores. The arrival of the railroad in 1832 established new commerce, with tanneries becoming a most common sight. In the late 1830s, financial stress led to the closing of many of the village businesses and the area did not rebound until many years later when it again began to flourish as a farming town. The most recent census indicates there are slightly more than 1500 residents.

Angenette B.S. Haight

The Cornell Family

The village's most celebrated personality is Ezra Cornell, the founder of Western Union and the co-founder of Cornell University. Born in the Bronx, in 1807, Cornell's parents raised him in DeRuyter. As a young man, he moved to Ithaca and took up carpentry. There many recognized him for his skill and dedication and Colonel Beebe elevated him to the position of mill manager. His subsequent marriage to a Methodist woman, Mary Ann Wood, resulted in his expulsion from the Quaker group to which he belonged, the Society of Friends.

With a family and his financial responsibility growing, Cornell quit the mill and took to selling a field plow for which he owned the patent. During his sales travel, he met an acquaintance of Samuel Morse which led to his involvement in the telegraph business. Working as an associate of Mr. Morse himself, Cornell ultimately amassed an impressive fortune. He made possible the stringing of telegraph lines along poles, coming up with the idea of using glass insulation to solve the connection issues. He became the president of the company in 1849.

From 1862 to 1867, Cornell served in both the New York State Assembly and Senate. In 1862, following his retirement from Western Union for which he received two million shares in the company, Cornell became heavily involved in philanthropy, providing a generous endowment to the now Cornell Library. That same year he took advantage of an available grant and established the university that would, in 1865, be granted a charter and which to this day carries his name.

In the late 1870s, Ezra started construction on a mansion in Ithaca. He called in Llenroc—his name spelled backwards. He died before its completion. The mansion is today home of the Delta Phi fraternity. Ezra Cornell currently rests in perpetuity in Sage Chapel on the university grounds.

We now come to the story of the decidedly more infamous Angenette B.S. Haight.

The Murder of George Haight

On February 27, 1883, at three o'clock in the morning, George Haight was lying asleep in his bed in DeRuyter, New York, when his wife Angenette put a bullet in his head. The shot did not kill him instantly and instead he managed to linger on a few weeks longer, eventually succumbing to the fatal wound while resting semi-consciously at the house of his uncle.

In a statement George made to the authorities prior to his death, he explained that he and his wife had retired at the usual time that evening, around 9:00, but he had awakened at two a.m., disturbed by the actions of Angenette. She explained to him she was suffering from a bout of rheumatism and could not sleep herself. He recalled he had waited on her for a short period of time but then returned to bed and fell asleep. His wife remained awake, and seated in an easy chair.

Further along in his statement, Mr. Haight says he woke again at the fatal hour to see his wife approaching him as he lay. She had in her hand a cloth from beneath which she produced a revolver. She then shot him. He recalled falling from the bed to the floor where he regained consciousness some time later. He managed to get himself back into the bed and called for the doctor.

A .22 caliber Smith and Wesson handgun, of which Mr. Haight claimed ownership, produced his wound. He said it was kept in the drawer of his night table, but by his recollection it contained no bullets. In the final part of his statement, he claimed his wife had no reason he knew of to do him harm and that his statement was true, made of sound mind and he was well aware he would soon die as the result of the injury to his brain.[1] He subsequently died on March 30th.

For her part, Angenette proclaimed her innocence and suggested her husband had tried to commit suicide, although she provided no motive. She claimed his statement as to her attempt to murder him developed due to an unsound mind as a result of his self-inflicted wound—which she had at one time claimed was not at all a bullet wound, but the result of him hitting his head on the bedpost.

Police eventually arrested Mrs. Haight and permitted her a period of time to dispose of her physical possessions before they incarcerated her. She remained in jail for almost one full year before she was tried.

Angenette B.S. Haight

On February 25, 1884, in Morrisville, Madison County, following a trial that lasted two full weeks and "generated greater interest than any murder trial that was ever held in the State of New York",[2] a jury found Mrs. Haight guilty of murder. One observer, describing her as she stood to hear the verdict, wrote: For a moment she stood in the dock a picture of grace, her snow-white hair carefully smoothed from the pallid brow and her slender hands clasped before her.[3]

Following the reading of the verdict, Justice Murray, the presiding judge, said, "Everything human has been done for you … you should not take any delusive hope … give yourself up to repentance. There is no chance for a new trial."[4] The judge sentenced her to be hung by the neck until dead on April 18th of that same year. She was sixty-two years of age.

During the trial, evidence revealed Mr. Haight held an insurance policy worth $25,000 with his wife listed as the sole beneficiary. Seemingly, she profited from similar policies taken out by her first two husbands and her own father, all of who died of unnatural causes.

The Background Story

Angenette was born Angenette Bump. Her father owned and operated a grist mill in Waterville, near Manlius. He sold the business in 1864 and went to live with Angenette, who had married her first husband, a Mr. Edgerton. During the two years he lived with her, Mr. Edgerton fell ill and doctors required him to go south for a while. Shortly after his return, he died under mysterious circumstances. Angenette relocated to Delphi and her mother soon joined her. Within six weeks of the move, her mother and father both died; again under unexplained circumstances Angenette also had three children. They, too, all died in young age, in or around 1867.

Cyrus Wood, also from DeRuyter, became Angenette's second husband. He died less than a year after their marriage, leaving his wife a substantial insurance policy. His relatives suspected he was poisoned.

Despite the general opposition of his friends and family—many knowing the fate of her previous husbands—George Haight became husband number three.

Shortly after their marriage, Angenette encouraged George to take out a life insurance policy, and he did, securing several, in fact, for a total of $18,000 in death benefits.[5] His wife's continued insistence on increasing the policies made George suspicious. He, in turn, decided not to keep up with the premiums, only to discover later that Angenette submitted the missed payments for him.

Becoming somewhat concerned about his wife's intentions, George secured employment in some capacity as a traveling agent and managed to stay on the road for extended periods of time. When he did come home, he went so far as to avoid drinking the daily cups of tea his wife would prepare for him, afraid they may be laced with poison. Despite his growing paranoia, he continued to live in the home.

As Angenette's bouts with rheumatism worsened, the couple hired a servant, Mrs. Abbey Salisbury, to both help with the house work and see to Angenette's care when warranted. The servant heard the fateful shot. She ran to the room and discovered Angenette standing over her husband looking at the bullet hole in the side of his head. According to her testimony, the lady of the house "seemed but little alarmed ... and did not desire a physician to be called."[6] She called one anyway. She also testified during the trial, that when she made the couples bed, she found beneath Angenette's pillow a revolver wrapped in a cloth.[7]

Ultimately, suspicions of foul play were confirmed when instead of showing concern for her husband, Angenette instead insisted on the insurance company's immediate response to fulfilling the terms of her late husband's policies.

Angenette's Fate

In an article appearing in the *New York Times* on April 11, 1884, the then Governor of New York State, Grover Cleveland, the soon to be President, granted clemency to Angenette B.S. Haight and commuted her sentence to life in the Onondaga State Penitentiary. In his statement of cause, the Governor acknowledged the heinous nature of the crime, while at the same time acknowledged the repugnance of hanging a woman and his lack of willingness to do so. He claimed he made his decision based solely on Angenette's advanced age and physical state of infirmary, declaring that reports made available to him indicated she would live but a short time longer.

George's brother, Jerome, in a statement he issued publically, admonished the Governor for his long-winded explanation, suggesting its content essentially provided old, infirm ladies license to commit murder. As for his assessment of her life span, he countered that for all anyone knew, she could live to the age of 100 and the people of the state would be required to provide for her upkeep for the duration.

The *Rochester Post-Express* called Angenette "hangable" and guilty of a series of murders "unrelieved of any feature of romance or passion".[8]

There is no available resource which provides for Angenette's death or for any reason to believe she lived a long life and died anywhere else but in prison.

Victims-7

Chapter 5
Polly Frisch

The lands that make up Genesee County once sat beneath the surface of a glacier formed body of water called Lake Tonawanda. At the time supplied by the waters of a much greater elevated Lake Erie, Lake Tonawanda itself spilled from a series of water falls into Lake Ontario. After the water level of Lake Erie receded, Lake Tonawanda dried up.

In 1959, while using a backhoe to deepen a pond on their property, once part of Lake Tonawanda, a family by the name of Hiscock discovered the tusk of a mastodon. Since then, the family donated 10 acres—named the Hiscock Site—to the Buffalo Museum of Science. Excavation has been on-going since 1986 and continues to yield prehistoric remains and Paleo-Indian artifacts.

Scientists traced these first artifacts—spearheads and other sharpened stones—back 11,000 years and believe that Paleo-Indians, who trailed game down from the far north, left the relics. In more recent history, around the 18th century, the Seneca tribe of the Iroquois Nation primarily populated the area. They settled along the Tonawanda Creek in what is now the city of Batavia.[1]

By the end of the century, however, in order to make way for settlers, the Big Tree Treaty drove the Seneca from the area and forced them onto reservation land. Alabama, New York is today home of the Tonawanda Indian Reservation.

Following the removal of the Seneca, three major investors divided the land into large tracts. The largest of these investors was a Dutch holding company by the name of the Holland Land Company, owned and operated by bankers from Amsterdam, Holland. They controlled over three million acres. They later sold the land in 1802 and it officially became Genesee County. Officials then divided the county into four townships with Batavia, by far, being the largest. They named the other three, all to the east, Northampton, Southampton and Leicester. Locals established the first recognized settlement in Oakfield on a plot of land that once held an Indian village.

Due to its rich soil and ideal climate, Genesee was, and still is primarily a rural, agricultural district made up of farms, pastures and in some regions ore and coal mines. The county built its first school house 1801. A gentleman from Rhode Island named Charles Wilber settled the town of LeRoy where, in 1857, the first university for women in the United States, Ingham University, was established. The region also became home to numerous seminaries and the New York State School of the Blind, which opened in 1865.

Notable Personalities

Throughout its history, Genesee has been the birthplace and home of numerous well-known and notable persons. Judge Francis A. Macomber, once a member of the Supreme Court, was born in Alabama, NY, in 1837. Daniel W. Powers, born in Batavia in 1818, is generally credited with the founding of Rochester.

Ira Edwin Leonard lived in Batavia before relocating to Las Vegas for health reasons. While there, he served as the defense attorney for the famous outlaw Billy the Kid. He managed to get the case dismissed, but Pat Garret shot Billy to death less than two months later.

Mina May Whiting Griswold, who lived in Darien, many believe to be the very first woman mail carrier in the United States. She came about the job by substituting for her husband after he fell ill and could not manage it himself. His job provided the only money for supporting her family.

Pearle Bixby Wait, from LeRoy, invented Jell-O in 1898. He originally worked in pharmaceuticals.

Ely Samuel Parker, a Seneca Indian, was born in Pembroke in 1828. He received his education from mission schools and later pursued a degree in law, only to be thwarted by a Supreme Court decision that declared Native Americans "non-citizens". Ultimately, he played a key role in the Civil War and is credited with transcribing the articles of surrender at Appomattox.

Ulysses S. Grant later appointed him as Commissioner of Indian Affairs. He passed away in 1895, having completed his professional career as a member of the New York City Police Department.

In more recent history, Oakfield is the birthplace of Katie Brownell. In 2005, she became the first girl to throw a perfect game in Little League Baseball, striking out every batter she faced—all boys. Her jersey hangs in the Baseball Hall of Fame in Cooperstown, NY.

This brings us to a story of a different sort, one of infamy and murder.

The Heinous Tale of Polly Frisch

The tale of Polly Frisch took place in Alabama in Genesee County, New York, around 1855. There is little known about Polly's early life other than she was born in 1825 and her mother went by the name of Maria Barbara Franklin.

Prior to the time she became of interest to the authorities, she lived life as a relative unknown, having married Henry Hoag in 1844. She also, unknown to her husband and the town's people, indulged in an affair with another man. Apparently, this other man had no love for children, and Polly and Henry had four of them (some sources indicate as many as six). She desired to remain in her illicit relationship and knew she must find a way to alter her situation.

As circumstance would have it, the town held an election party, a sort of county fair, locally. While attending, Polly decided to visit a clairvoyant to obtain her fortune. It foretold the deaths of two family members, but assured her that she would not to be one of them. Allowing her imagination—some say insanity—to get the better of her, she used the opportunity to conjure up a diabolical idea of her own to eliminate the obstacles that stood before her and her lover.[2]

Henry would be the first obstacle to be removed. Less than a year after the fortune telling, July of 1856, Polly killed her husband by poisoning him with arsenic. The local authorities suspected foul play, but given the science and technology of the time combined with the rural setting, they never followed-up. That left Polly free to move forward with phase two of her plan—the elimination of her children.

Less than one week after disposing of Henry, the couple's six-year old daughter, Frances, fell ill. She died only twenty-four hours later. Apparently,

44

she ate bread and butter and drank tea, all of which had been sprinkled with arsenic. Again, police suspected wrongdoing, but never ordered a formal autopsy or investigation.

Polly's attempts at doing away with her other two children, nine year old Albert and seven year old Rosealie, thankfully failed, and she instead sent them to live with relatives.

All her efforts, however, were for naught, as her lover, who remains to this day anonymous, decided he didn't want anything to do with her and left.

In the winter of 1857, Polly married a man by the name of Otto Frisch. Polly poisoned him a short time after, but he managed to survive and fled to Canada. That October, Polly spiked her 21 month-old daughter's porridge with arsenic and the girl, Eliza Jane, died.

But this death was a bit too coincidental for a counselor by the name of S. E. Filkins. He demanded an investigation.[3]

Police arrested Polly Frisch in Alabama on November 9, 1857 and charged her with the death of her first husband, Henry Hoag. On or about July 8 of the following year, she was tried in a court in Genesee County and acquitted of the charge.[4] Prosecutors subsequently charged her with the murders of two of her children. Authorities held her in a jail in Batavia.

The morgue sent the youngest child's stomach for examination. However, by the time the pathologist received the organ it was in no condition to yield positive and conclusive results. Nonetheless, the chemist concluded, given the proximity of the largely unexplained deaths, that foul play was probable. He convinced the local authorities to exhume and examine the bodies of the family members. The remains all bore the presence of arsenic.

Following her arrest, Polly Frisch admitted to poisoning her older child, but proclaimed her actions as accidental. Ultimately, a jury found her guilty of killing not only her first husband but her children as well.

Polly remained incarcerated in the jail in Batavia until her trial commenced late in the summer of 1859. Altogether, she sat through four trials, the last of which took place in September of that year. Following deliberation, the jury found her guilty of premeditated murder for the death of Frances and sentenced her to die by hanging. Her execution, scheduled for November 2nd, would make her the first woman in the history of Genesee to die on the gallows.

The Man Who Was Hanged Twice

From a historical perspective, the first execution by hanging in Genesee County took place in 1807. A court found a man by the name of James McLean guilty of killing two local men with an axe. The killing took place in or near a tavern by the name of The Springs located in Caledonia, which was previously known as Southampton.

According to the details, McLean and two other men, Archibald MacLachlan and William Orr, drank brandy, a common day time routine of the period, and were likely in a drunkard state which contributed to the violence to come. McLean and Orr started arguing about the felling of some trees to which McLean was partial. In response McLean hit him a number of times with an axe, including twice in the throat, killing him instantly. MacLachlan attempted to come to Orr's aid when McLean struck him also in the back and the blade of the axe cleaved his heart.

McLean fled into the dense woods, but a local woman and her son witnessed both his crime as well as his escape route. Police captured him a number of days later and held him at the jail in Batavia. Later they tried and sentenced him to hang. As the story goes, the day of his execution, the rope around his neck snapped and McLean fell to the ground stunned but very much alive. Some of those assembled argued he should be let free, as the letter of the law had been carried out. Others, however, felt since he murdered two men, he should hang twice. The second time, the rope did its job.

Available records show only six or seven executions have been carried out in Genesee County since the hanging of James McLean.

As for Polly Frisch, shortly after her sentencing, the then Governor of New York State, Edwin D. Morgan, made an application for clemency based on a claim of insanity due to epilepsy. Pharmaceutical companies introduced the first effective anti-seizure medicine in the mid-1800s, but many still considered the affliction to be a form of mental incapacity. In some parts of the world, believers thought those afflicted to be possessed by demons or some other form of evil spirit. Morgan was well-known for his charitable contributions and particularly to the Union Theological Seminary. It would not be consistent with his character to permit a woman to die in such a way. Based on expert testimony the application was granted. A judge commuted

Polly Frisch

Polly's sentence to life in prison.

Frisch began serving her sentence in Sing-Sing prison in 1859, located on the east bank of the Hudson River in the village of Ossining. Contrary to popular belief, the facility was named not for the village, but for the Sint Sinck, the Indian people from which the original settlers purchased the land. The state then transferred her to Kings County Penitentiary. The institution was located in Brooklyn, in a section called Crow Hill, between Flatbush and Bedford. A tall stone fence surrounded the penitentiary which included a workhouse. The prison housed both men and women, most of who had been convicted of misdemeanors and petty crime, in different units. Polly spent the next 33 years there. During her time, she worked in the prison hospital and earned a reputation as a dedicated and caring health care provider. The state demolished the prison in 1907.

In December of 1892, the 30th Governor of the State of New York, Roswell Pettibone Flower, given assurances by Dr. Homer L. Bartlett that Frisch was fully rehabilitated and no longer suffering from any form of insanity, pardoned her.

Frisch, known to those in the prison as Aunt Polly, received word of her pardon from Warden Hayes and her long-time attorney, Foster L. Backus. When informed of her release, she was purported to have said, "Thank you, sir; thank God, sir. I will now be able to spend the rest of my days out of prison."[5]

"Old and feeble", Frisch remained in the Brooklyn, New York area, where she lived with and cared for an old friend. It is assumed that after her passing due to old age—her age believed to be 75, Polly was buried locally. There is no information as to the actual date of her death or the cemetery in which she was interred.

Victims-3

Chapter 6

Frances Shrouder

Chittenango is a village in Madison County, New York. It is located less than ten miles south of Oneida Lake and about 15 miles east of Syracuse. The Erie Canal system runs through the north side of the village. The village gets its name from the Oneida word for "where the sun shines out". Villagers first called it Chittening.

Settlers first came to Chittenango in the early 19th century and recognized it as a village in 1812. Residents built the first homes along the Great Genesee Road and the Chittenango Creek, which runs north to south through the middle of the village. The earliest settlers cultivated the land and depended on the creek as both a source of water and for power. The element gypsum filled the hills in the area which led John B. Yates to found of one of its first commercial enterprises, a plaster mill for the manufacturing of cement. The mill and its product played a significant role in the building of the Erie Canal.

Construction of the Erie Canal reached Chittenango in 1820. A second canal, or Lateral Canal, known as the Chittenango Canal Boat Landing, extended into the middle of the village in 1855, opening up transportation as far east as the Hudson River and as far west as the Great Lakes. The area grew posthaste as a result, with services and establishments geared towards those passing through, such as hotels, inns and eateries. Towards the end of the century, 1897, the Chittenango Pottery Company opened on the banks of the Erie Canal with the hopes of competing with products coming out of China. While it did have some early success, producing some collectable pieces shown at the Buffalo Exposition of 1901, the company experienced two serious fires, and after rebuilding, ceased operation in 1920.

Notable People

By far, the most famous personality from the Chittenango was L. Frank Baum; author of *The Wonderful Wizard of Oz*. Born in 1856, Baum's parents were devout Methodists. His father was a wealthy businessman who produced barrels for transporting oil. Baum received his early education at home and then attended two years at the Peekskill Military Academy. He began his writing career soon after, producing two different local journals. The George M. Hill Company published *The Wizard of Oz* in 1900 and it became an immediate success, spending two consecutive years as a best seller and providing him with significant earnings. He would go on to write and publish 13 subsequent works all based on the characters and setting of the original story. He died in 1919 while residing in California.

John Kirby Allen was born in Canaseraga Village, which is now known as Sullivan County. At age 16, he formed a business partnership with a friend and opened a store in Chittenango selling hats. He cashed in his interest in the store in 1827 and moved with his brother to New York City where they became involved as investors. In 1833 the brothers moved to Texas and played a peripheral role in the Texas Revolution. In 1836, while serving as a Representative for the County of Nacogdoches, he and his brother founded the city of Houston which he then successfully lobbied to have declared the capital of the Republic. He died of congestive fever two years later.

This brings us to the story of the less reputable Frances Shrouder.

Murderess

The *Chicago Daily Tribune* reported the story of Frances Shrouder on October 21, 1879. The article, which first appeared in the *Cincinnati Inquirer*, was titled "A Startling Story."[1] According to the details, police arrested Frances and her husband, George, under order of Justice Bettinger for the murder of

Mrs. Laney Barnard, a 60 year-old widow living in Chittenango, New York, and the mother of Frances.

The actual tale begins in April of 1876. Frances had a great aunt by the name of Mrs. Louisa Pope. She lived alone on a piece of property which she owned in Truxton, in Cortland County. Frances' father, Charles Barnard, made arrangements for Mrs. Pope to come and live with the Barnards in their home.

Upon her arrival in Chittenango, most people knew that Mrs. Pope had in her possession $800 in bonds and that she held a $1000 mortgage on her property in Truxton, altogether a tidy sum in the 19th century. She intended to use the money as a means of supporting herself for the rest of her life, which as it turned out, would be shorter than she had anticipated.

Just three months after moving in with the Barnards, Mrs. Pope became ill without warning. She complained of pain throughout her body and suffered from violent spasms and other symptoms which indicated poisoning. She died on a Saturday on the last weekend in July.

No sooner had her body grown cold and even before rigor mortis set in, Charles arranged for Mr. Greminger, the village undertaker, to have a cheap coffin fashioned. The undertaker soon after sealed the body of Mrs. Pope inside and permitted no one to view the body. No local services marked her passing.

The next morning, on Sunday, Charles loaded the coffin onto a wagon and carried the body back to Truxton where he insisted Mrs. Pope's remains be laid to rest without delay. No more than six hours elapsed from the time of death to burial.

Following her great aunt's passing, many often observed Frances Shrouder in the possession of an inordinate amount of cash, many a time asking to have bills of large denomination changed at the local stores. To account for the sudden appearance of wealth, her father, Charles, made it known that he and his family, the sole surviving relatives of Mrs. Pope, had been made by default the beneficiaries of her remaining estate. The matter went uncontested as no one had cause to gainsay the claim. However, a will did turn up at a later time which expressed Mrs. Pope's wish for her estate to go to the Presbyterian Board of Home Missions.[2]

As it turns out, Frances had poisoned Mrs. Pope with the motive of taking possession of the cash bonds. As compensation for his role—covering for his daughter's actions and removing the evidence—her father made claim to the mortgage. He did not remain in possession of it for long.

Frances Shrouder

Two years later, with the cash bonds running low, George Shrouder convinced Frances they would be better off with Charles no longer in the picture. He died of suspicious circumstances soon after, leaving only Frances' mother Laney as an obstacle to the mortgage and the Barnard property.

When Frances' mother died on September 28th of the following year, the circumstances of her death, placed within the context of the events prior, appeared too coincidental to the authorities. At the request of the coroner, Mrs. Barnard's body was handed over to the medical examiner, Dr. William Manlius Smith. During the postmortem, Dr. Smith discovered the presence of arsenic in her stomach, "but not yet in quantities sufficient to cause death."[3] The testimony to follow, however, indicated that just prior to her passing, Mrs. Barnard vomited with considerable force, thereby expelling most of the contents of her stomach, including the arsenic. Further investigation revealed that not long ago Frances had purchased the poison from a local drug store.

As a result of the findings, police exhumed Charles' body, as well as the remains of Mrs. Pope. Prosecutors scheduled a coroner's jury for October 27th to take place in Wheeler's Hotel in Portland County.

Until that date, police remanded the two suspects to the Madison County Jail. The authorities felt confident that Frances, who many described as weak-minded, would confess her role in the murder of her great aunt, her father and mother, and provide testimony she did so at the urging of her husband. They believed George would, in order to spare himself the sentence of execution by hanging, then confess his role, as well. However, George Merwin, the village policeman assigned to the jail, reported that Mr. Shrouder, while incarcerated, made the statement it would not be he who would suffer from the crime. When asked who would, he stated, "Well, I won't." —meaning he intended his wife to take the blame.[4]

A Modern Day Lucrezia Borgia

At the time of her arrest, print media referred to Frances Shrouder as a modern day Borgia. Almost twenty years earlier, they also gave Elizabeth P. McCraney the same title. In both cases, the name refers to Lucrezia Borgia, a historical *femme fatale* whose love interests more often than not met with unnatural deaths for which she was, to at least some degree, accountable.

Lucrezia Borgia, born in 1480, was the daughter of Pope Alexander VI. Seeking political alliances, her father arranged two marriages for the then 11 year-old Lucrezia. Lucky for her, circumstance called off each marriage before consummation. However, at the age of 13 she did formally wed Giovanni Sforza. Shortly after the marriage, though, her father changed his mind, seeking stronger alliances, and sought to have their arrangement annulled. Sforza objected and therefore became a target of assassination by Lucrezia's brother, Cesare. He fled and ultimately agreed to sign the papers in exchange for the dowry.

While separated from her husband, Lucrezia engaged in an affair with a member of her father's court by the name of Pedro Calderon. Locals later found Pedro dead and floating in the Tiber River. No one could ever verify the rumor of the affair. Less than a year later, however, a child was born to the Borgia household. Though many believed the child to be that of Pedro and Lucrezia her brother claimed the bastard child as his own.

In 1498, Lucrezia married her second husband, Alfonso of Aragon. He expected to be named governor of Spoleto, but instead the title went to Lucrezia. Alfonso fled Rome but made the mistake of returning at his wife's request and was killed soon after. Citizens believed he, too, was killed by Cesare, as the brother had aligned himself with France and against Naples.

Lucrezia married for a third time in 1502. Though neither she nor her husband, Alfonso I d'Este, remained faithful during their marriage—she had multiple affairs, both with her brother-in-law and the poet, Pietro Bembo—Alfonso did manage to survive the marriage. He died in 1534, 15 years after the death of Lucrezia, who died giving birth to her eighth child.

Victims-3

Chapter 7

Caroline D. Sorgenfrie

Rome is located in north-central New York not far Syracuse and directly east of Lake Ontario. Delta Lake is to its north, and the much larger Lake Oneida to its west. The city is connected to the New York State Thruway by Route 49 which runs west north-west. The city is part of the Mohawk Valley.

A hundred years or more before the state formally recognized city of Rome, the area was the site of the only overland route between water ways to the east from the direction of the Hudson River and those to the west that led to Lake Ontario. At the time called the Oneida Carrying Place, workers required those merchants ferrying goods in either direction to off-load their cargo, transport it across open land, and then load it again on another boat on the other end. The original settlements served as fortifications to defend the Carrying Place and protect the merchants from Indian raiding parties and highway robbers.

Fort Stanwix became the most acclaimed of these fortifications, built just north of the banks of the Mohawk River. Manned by the British during the French and Indian War, which began in 1754, Fort Stanwix served to stem the Native American activity in the area, most of whom supported the French. No longer relevant once the French abandoned their efforts in the colonies to concentrate on their European enemies, the British left Fort Stanwix in 1777, and settlers tore down the fort to use the material for their own buildings.

The area once again became a focal point during the Revolutionary War when Fort Stanwix was again rebuilt, but this time by the local militia fighting against the British. Fortified by members of the Oneida natives, together they manned the fort and managed to repel a sustained siege by the British. After the British forces gave up the fight and retreated, the Oneida left and joined the loyalists who had been reinforced by members of the Iroquois and Mohawk Tribes. Together they attacked and killed unsuspecting settlers.

In response to their slaughter, General George Washington ordered the militia still stationed at Fort Stanwix to pursue and drive the enemy from the valley. The Sullivan Expedition of 1779 became the most notorious of these campaigns, which had as its goal the utter destruction of those of the Iroquois Nation who fought alongside the British. The ruthlessness of their efforts, combined with tribal in-fighting, resulted in the annihilation of more than 50 villages and their inhabitants. The surviving natives fled to Canada. In 1781, settlers again abandoned and razed the fort as they no longer needed it.

In 1796, with peace returning to the area, the construction of the Rome Canal began. As a result, the settlement experienced significant growth and locals formed. The Erie Canal expanded to Rome in 1817, running along the southern edge of the city where the Mohawk River joined it east of the city's center. The waterways combined solidified Rome as an important cog in the east-west trade route and provided a means for making the area's natural resources available to the rest of the country. An act of the New York State Legislature incorporated Rome in 1870.

Today, Rome is a city of approximately 35,000 people and its location serves as one of the only remaining inland Pine Barrens in the United States.

Free Love

Francis Bellamy, the author of *The Pledge of Allegiance*, lived in Rome. Born in Mount Morris, Mr. Bellamy moved with his family to Rome in 1890. His father found employment as a minister in the First Baptist Church, and Francis soon followed in his footsteps. A graduate of the University of Rochester, his dedication to the church eventually brought him to Massachusetts where, while writing for a patriotic circular called the *Youth's Campaign*, he wrote *The Pledge of Allegiance*. Although Bellamy spent most of his later years living in Florida, following his death in 1931, his remains were cremated and buried in the family plot in Rome.

Caroline D. Sorgenfrie

John Humphrey Noyes, another man of the cloth, also associated himself with Oneida County. Born in Vermont in 1811, Noyes decided on a career in the ministry at the age of 20. He entered the Yale Theological Seminary to study the bible. Particularly interested in predicting the time of the Second Coming, he came to the personal realization that it had already passed, identifying the date as 70 A.D.

Obsessed with the concepts of salvation from sin and perfectionism, Noyes came to the conclusion that one could not only be free of sin, but man could not sin at all given that man's will came from God and as such was divine. He became further convinced that God intended man to live by his intuition. His views and willingness to speak openly about them ultimately resulted in his expulsion from the ministry. As a result, he left Vermont and came to Oneida in 1848 where he established a commune of like-minded people called the Oneida Community.

Community members practiced free love, including sex between consenting persons. There were no marital boundaries, sex often occurred between menopausal women and adolescent boys and mature men and younger girls. People in the community held open criticism in public forums designed to expose the faults of an individual. They also designed a selective breeding program, stirpiculture, created for the perfection of children based on specific criteria.

Following Noyes' departure in 1879—he fled to Canada ahead of a warrant for his arrest charging him with adultery—the commune slowly deteriorated with its youngest members desiring a more traditional life style. Noyes died in Ontario in 1886. He was buried in Oneida.

Pat Riley, one of the premier basketball coaches in the history of the NBA, was born in Rome in 1945. His family would move to Schenectady where Pat spent his childhood. He attended Linton High School where he participated in one of the greatest high school games in the State's history. In 1961, Linton High School defeated New York City's Power Memorial along with their star player, Lew Alcindor, better known as Kareem Abdul-Jabbar, one of the greatest players in NBA history. Ironically, Riley would go on to coach Abdul-Jabbar as a member of the Los Angeles Lakers.

Although Riley would go on to have a brief and unremarkable career as an NBA player, he is better recognized for his exploits as both a coach and central office figure of multiple teams. Currently working with the Miami

Heat, he won five NBA championships as a coach and 2 as an executive. He no doubt will eventually be selected to the NBA Hall of Fame.

Alex Haley, best credited for his work *Roots*, was a long-time resident of Rome. Born in Ithaca, he moved to Tennessee as a child, but returned to New York at the age of 5. Alex enrolled in Alcorn State University in Mississippi at the age of 15. The next year he transferred to Elizabeth City State College in North Carolina. He dropped out at the end of the year and returned to Ithaca where his father insisted he join the Coast Guard. He served for the next twenty years. In 1949, following World War II, he became a journalist for the Coast Guard and served at that position until he retired from military service ten years later.

As a civilian, Haley took a job with the Reader's Digest and later became a senior editor. In 1965, Haley, after more than 50 interviews with Malcolm X, most of which he found to be arduous and frustrating due to his subjects stubbornness, published, as a ghost writer, *The Autobiography of Malcolm X*. In 1998, the book was named one of the ten most influential non-fiction books of the twentieth century.

Doubleday published *Roots: the Saga of an American Family* in 1976. Haley intended the book to be autobiographical in nature, insisting that the story contained the true history of his family's forced arrival to this country. It tells the tale of Kunta Kinte who was taken from his homeland of Gambia and sold as a slave in Maryland. The work won Haley a Pulitzer Prize in 1977 and producers turned it into a television mini-series seen by more than 100 million viewers. In 1978, Harold Courlander accused Haley of plagiarism with regard to his work and sued him. Following a five week trial, the two parties reached a settlement, part of which required Haley to acknowledge the fictional nature of the work.

Black Widow

In 1838, Caroline Wilsey was born in Dearfield, a village in Utica. She first married a man named James Staley. Together they had two children. In 1861, Mr. Staley became the victim of unfortunate circumstance, falling from Potter's Bridge, a covered structure spanning the dyke that made up part of the canal system joining the town to the Mohawk River, and to water below. He

Caroline D. Sorgenfrie

drowned. While no witnesses accounted for how Mr. Staley managed to fall into the water, rumors circulated that he may have been pushed by Mrs. Staley.

Mrs. Staley then became Mrs. Henry Way. The only information about Mr. Way is that he left to serve in the Civil War and never returned. Whether he thought muskets and canon fire was the safer alternative than to continue his relationship with Mrs. Way has not been determined.

In 1881, at the age of 43, Mrs. Way again legally changed her name. She married the then 76 year-old Ernest W. Schroeder. They enjoyed wedded bliss for less than two years, when one morning Mr. Schroeder found his breakfast pork to be especially disagreeable. He summoned a physician to attend to his malady, but to little avail. He died later that evening. The subsequent autopsy discovered the presence of arsenic in his stomach, but no one called for a formal inquest.

And this brings the story to John Sorgenfrie, a gentleman of Germen descent. Following the unexpected passing of husband number three, Mrs. Schroeder started a relationship with future husband number four. Prior to formalizing their relationship, Mr. Sorgenfrie lived in Caroline's residence on Laurel Street (a short distance from where Ft. Stanwix once stood) in Rome as a boarder. This he did for two years. No doubt smitten, he proposed to his landlord and offered, as a dowry, property of his that he valued at $2000. They married in 1883.

Their marriage, however, was neither one of bliss or fidelity. The couple often had harsh words for each other, and for a period of time, Mr. Sorgenfrie moved from the home. Following his return, their relationship remained similarly contrary. One particular evening, in fact, Mrs. Sorgenfrie found her husband in the company of a woman with compromised reputation by the name of Ms. Fox.[1] To make matters worse, the lady informed the woman of the house that she, too, would be moving in to share the couples' living space. Mr. Sorgenfrie died less than a week later.

On the morning of May 26, at approximately 6 a.m., John Sorgenfrie was found dead in his bed. He was sixty years-old at the time. When interviewed by the authorities, Mrs. Sorgenfrie professed complete surprise, stating only that he had enjoyed a large meal the night prior. Authorities noted at the time, however, that ample evidence of Paris Green could be found about the house. It is a highly toxic inorganic compound similar to arsenic and is used for pest control and as a coloring agent due to its green tint.

Initially, the coroner entertained the idea of Mr. Sorgenfrie committing suicide, but following the questioning of Mrs. Sorgenfrie's sons and the widow herself, he found too many contradictions in their stories. Police arrested Mrs. Sorgenfrie and charged her with the poisoning and murder of poor old John. They remanded her to the jail in Utica. In her defense, she stated that on the night before his death he had returned to the home under the influence of alcohol, refused to eat his supper—an obvious contradiction to her previous statement—and threatened to kill her. He said, "I got full to kill you". Subsequent to Caroline being indicted by a grand jury, unbelievably, any record of Caroline Sorgenfrie disappeared from history. We can only hope she at least didn't remarry!

Victims-4

BABY FARMERS

Chapter 8

Margaret McCloskey

Manhattan, like many of the urban cities in the north east, experienced exponential growth throughout the 19th century, but particularly so starting about 1850. The Germans, Italians, and in particular, the Irish contributed to this population explosion. The Great Hunger, better known to some as the potato famine, struck Ireland in 1845, and by the time the dust settled in 1852, almost half the Irish population immigrated, with a significant percentage coming into New York Harbor and up the East River.

Penniless and with little prospect for work beyond physical labor, if it existed, most Irish gathered in the poorest quarters in the city, with the worst area being a densely packed section known as the Five Points.

Life in the Five Points was brutal. Originally destined to be an upper-middle class neighborhood, planners constructed the single family homes, modest apartment complexes and businesses over a landfill which in short time decayed. As a result, the buildings and streets sunk below water level, backing up the sewer systems and flooding with the rains. As the filth and disease became inescapable, the original residents and business owners abandoned the area and took their money with them.

The fate of the Five Points was sealed when the Old Brewery, a huge building sitting at the heart of the intersecting streets, came to be taken over by unscrupulous sorts, converted into a tenement building and filled with the poorest of the poor. In due time, the area gained the distinction of the highest density in population n the western world.

By the time the Ladies Home Missionary Society razed the Old Brewery in 1852, the streets of the Five Points housed thousands of Street Arabs— children abandoned by their parents. Countless more children, with most being infants, were left by unwed or destitute mothers on the doorsteps of developing missions and local churches.

Well into the later years of the 19th century, services available for the protection of children were themselves in their infancy, with most of them having been established with donations and managed by well-meaning individuals and smaller organizations. Faced with little to no option, desperate mothers left their infants and children too young to fend for themselves in the streets, in the care of strangers, many of who saw a profit in the undertaking. These individuals, often women with no other means themselves, became known as *baby farmers*.

One of the most infamous of these women went by the name of Margaret McCloskey...

The Diabolical Tale of Margaret McCloskey

Margaret McCloskey, also known as Margaret McClinchy, resided in New York City in 1876. Due to the nature of her enterprise, she moved around quite often, and at the time of our story, lived as a tenant in two apartments on both East Twenty-Fifth Street and Second Avenue. She claimed the profession of wet nurse and used her homes to board infant children.

Had it not been for the attentiveness of a somewhat nosey neighbor, McCloskey may have continued to endanger the lives of the children for whom she provided supervision. That neighbor, Mrs. Elizabeth Clifford, of West Third Street, befriended a young woman by the name of Mrs. Catherine French. Mrs. French, already the mother of a fourteen month old infant, gave birth, only weeks before, to her second child. Unfortunately, just prior to the baby's birth, her husband abandoned her, leaving her without means of income. With no other choice, she herself took employment as a wet nurse and arranged to leave her children in the care of Mrs. McCloskey at her home for which she paid $18 per month.

From the first floor apartment which Mrs. McCloskey occupied only for a short period of time, Mrs. Clifford couldn't help but notice the constant sound of babies crying. Concerned for the two young children of her friend, she inquired throughout the area about the situation and heard rumors that many more children than just two lived in the apartment and that their caretaker severely neglected them. She made it her business to gain entrance wherein she found six infants, each of which appeared weak and sickly to the point of mortal peril. She informed the authorities at the Eighteenth Precinct.

Before long, Officer Alexander Gerner from the Society for the Prevention of Cruelty to Children, accompanied by an officer from the Eighteenth Precinct, made a formal visit to the house. The officer found three adult women in the apartment at the time of the visit, none of whom was Mrs. McCloskey. Two of the women, each cradling an infant in her arms, identified themselves as servants and provided their service in exchange for board. The other, Catherine Conklin, claimed to be a companion of Mrs. McCloskey; however, the authorities obtained reason to believe she played an active role in finding and convincing unwed and troubled mothers to leave their infants to the care of Mrs. McCloskey for a fee.

During this official visit, officers verified the accounts of Mrs. Clifford. The apartment housed six infants but only a single crib. The oldest appeared to be no more than three years of age, while the others happened to be only weeks or months old. No food or formula could be found in the apartment. Reports described the children as unclean and starving, their limbs and bodies skinny and emaciated.

Though no reports mention it, one of the children may have been the infant recently birthed by Mrs. French. Only a couple of days prior, while in the home to check on her two children, Mrs. French discovered her oldest to be unresponsive and in failing health. When she parted, she took the boy with her but there is no further mention of the newborn.

Mrs. McCloskey returned to the residence that evening and removed one of the infants. Prior to leaving, she arranged to have two other infants returned to their mothers. She again appeared at the house the following afternoon and police arrested her. They charged her and held her on $1000 bail in anticipation of a hearing. In her defense, she stated that she worked for some time as a wet nurse boarding infants and young children and always treated them well.

The Disposition of Margaret McCloskey

An article that appeared in the *New York Times* on July 2, 1876, reported that Mrs. McCloskey, referred to as Mrs. McClinchy, and described as being middle-age, of average height and thin build, with black hair and eyes, pled guilty to "cruelly neglecting children". In turn she received the relatively light sentence of six months in the penitentiary along with a fine of $250.[1]

The article, which is by and large an opinion piece, goes on to acknowledge the extent of the baby farming problem in the city. It attributes the phenomena to the many evils inherent in urban life and accuses the abandoning parents of wishing to have the children done away with. From the writer's perspective, the problem could be mitigated by providing harsher penalties to the likes of Margaret McCloskey who was referred to as an "instrument [of death]."

Victims-3, possibly more[2]

Chapter 9

Catherine Claus

M aspeth is a town in the borough of Queens, located in Long Island City on Long Island. It lies just east of the East River, across the river from Manhattan and just north of Brooklyn. The Dutch and the English first settled the area in 1642. They called the first settlement Maspat, a derivation of the name of the Indians native to the area, the Mespeatches. The name, loosely translated, meant "place of bad water"—owing to the many swamps in the area. However, the Indians attacked and wiped out that first settlement. Settlers returned years later and in greater numbers, eventually establishing the town of Newton, which today is called Elmhurst.

Swamp Land

James Maurice served as a United States Representative. Born in New York City in 1814, he became a clerk in a local law office at the age of 12. He was admitted to the bar in 1835, after which he moved to Maspeth to start his own practice. He worked as a member of the Assembly in 1851 and again in 1866. Voters then elected him to Congress and he served from 1853 to 1855. He was nominated to the Supreme Court in 1865, but declined and instead returned to his law practice in Maspeth.

In 1847, Maurice donated the land at Rust St. and 57th Dr. upon which crews built the St. Savior's Church. A proud local landmark, vandals torched the building in 1970. In 2006, the city dismantled the remains and placed the pieces in storage with the hope of re-erecting the church on park grounds which are yet to be purchased.

Maurice's home, which currently stands on its original property, 1 Hill Street, are only a small part of the land he held in the area. In addition, he owned considerable acreage, among which was a 72 acre tract of forest and swamp known as Maurice Woods. It became the final resting place of as many as fifteen infants left to die by Catherine Claus and her husband, Charles.

Earning a Living by Killing

The story of Catherine Claus begins in Long Island City in New York and ends in Maspeth, Queens, on Long Island. Catherine married Charles and together they had one child of their own, a son, Otto. Catherine, it turns out, had been baby farming for more than twenty years, and along with her husband, officials found the two responsible for the verified deaths of at least five children and probably many more.

When the authorities knocked on the couples' front door of their home in Maspeth, described both as a hovel and a hut in the woods, they entered to find two dead or dying infants. The first, found in an otherwise bare crib and hardly more than a few months old, had been starved to death. The second, somewhat older child, at that moment took the final breaths of life. Then alerted by the unmistakable odor of decay, police dismantled one of the beds to find the decomposing remains of a baby about two weeks of age concealed within the mess of feathers that made up the mattresses. They found the body black with decay, reeking and showing signs of being there two, perhaps three days. A coroner's examination suggested the child had been poisoned with opium but that suffocation was the final cause of death. He also revealed a strong presence of opium in the systems of the other two victims.[1]

Apparently, the couple, while living at 131 Webster Avenue in Ravenswood, Long Island City, attracted the attention of their neighbors by the number of young women entering the house with babies in their arms and exiting without them.[2] However, no one reported the activity until the locals in Long Island City, Woodside and Winfield began waking to crying babies abandoned on their doorstep. As a result, the couple's home came under surveillance by policemen from the First Precinct who suspected their involvement in baby farming.

The Clauses soon became aware of the attention and within the normal routine of their daily movement, packed their belongings into a one horse green wagon, and left the house. They moved to the home in Maspeth on Fisk Ave. Upon which Mr. Claus had yet to complete construction.[3] Authorities later described the home, located 500 feet off the road and in a thick wood, in the following passage:

> **It was a rough one-story-and-a-half house of unpainted wood. Part of the wood was second-hand stuff. The house was squalid and repulsive looking. Its floor stood four feet above the ground ... [no] attempt at a cellar or a foundation wall had been made. The house stood in a hollow at the top of a high piece of ground, but many springs nearby made the earth swampy.[4]**

Not more than a few days after taking up their new residence, someone left a baby outside the Dominican Sisters Home in Winfield. By chance a local judge by the name Brandon happened to pass the home, hearing an infant's cry. Unfortunately, despite his best efforts the neglected baby died.

Brandon decided to investigate the house. At one point he noted baby carriage tracks leading from the road up to the home. He arranged for Sergeant Thomas Darcy of the Newton Police to put the house under surveillance. At the same time the police chief assigned a second officer, Charles Emhoff, to monitor the train station for anyone suspicious of transporting babies.

In the course of this surveillance, an officer observed a New York woman by the name of Mrs. Karch getting off a train. She proceeded to ask for directions to the Claus Home. She carried with her an infant. During her walk, she became aware of the patrolman trailing her and she changed direction.[5] The officer, Constable Michael Quis of Winfield, followed her to Williamsburg where he endeavored to have the local police department take her into custody and hold her until formal charges could be brought. The desk officer, however, refused citing a lack of cause.

Police later discovered that Mrs. Karch had sent a telegram—in German—to Catherine and Charles suggesting they meet. Karch advertised herself as a professional nurse, and she supplied most of the infants to Claus. Brandon became aware of the telegram—news traveled fast in the small town—and he used it to track down an advertisement listed by Karch in a German language newspaper.

Over the next couple of weeks, a second baby was left abandoned in proximity to the Claus residence, this one in a soap box at the door of a local grocer, Theodore Christman. Charles later confessed his responsibility in abandoning no less than 40 babies throughout different locations over the previous fourteen months. He left the baby outside the grocer, and Mrs. Claus who deposited the other outside the Dominican Sisters Home. Reportedly, the couple had been paid anywhere from $1 to $4 to take the children.[6]

Following the discovery of the lifeless infants within the Claus house, the authorities suspected more bodies would be found. Toward the back of the home and property a shallow bog-like pond was concealed from the street by thick tree growth and dense foliage, known as Maurice Woods. Scum covered the surface of the pond and the water appeared dark and muddy. The pond was actually located on property owned by the Episcopal Diocese of Long Island, donated by James Maurice.

Relying upon the local fire department, Maspeth Steam Fire Engine Company 4, under the command of Foreman Monteverde, Justice McDonald Maspeth arranged to have a pump truck drain the pond.

County official Jeromus Rapelye, Superintendent of the Poor, discovered the first body toward the end of the initial day when he spotted a small bundle of cloth sunken into the mire. Quietly and without calling any attention to himself, he removed the bundle and carried it to a secluded spot. A crowd of locals gathered, estimated as many as 1000 and included enterprising peddlers selling lemonade and peanuts out of carts.[7] Out of sight of others, both those working at the grisly task and the locals, rapidly unwrapped the bundle and discovered the largely decomposed remains of a baby of no more than a month old. Two more bodies were uncovered before they completed the work, one of which had been stuffed into an iron kettle and weighed down by a five pound rock.

Police held the couple in a local jail in Newton and informed them they discovered the bodies of the discarded infants. Mrs. Claus, as "a hideous old hag ... [with] reddish brown hair, wrinkled and sallow skin and restless eyes that looked out over a long, thin nose and protrusive chin ... the picture of what anyone would imagine a professional child-killer looks like",[8] was reported to have said, "I've put away fifteen, but let them find them."[9] That evening, fearing for their safety from the rumor of gathering lynch mobs, police moved the couple to a jail in Long Island City.

Along with the Clauses, police arrested three mid-wives, Bertha Schroeder, Elizabeth Werner and Karch, and charged them with accessory for arranging to have children brought into the care of the baby farmers. Ultimately, Otto Claus, the son, became instrumental in obtaining the formal confession from his parents, perhaps something the couple agreed to do to remove him from suspicion of compliance.

On October 6, 1890, officers brought the pair from the jail in Long Island City to face charges of man slaughter, among others. To the surprise of those in the community, each received the relatively lenient sentence of ninety days in the county jail.[10] The judge fully exonerated Otto.

Victims 5, boasted of killing 15

Chapter 10
Cynthia McDonald

Rochester, formally established in 1834, is another city whose history sprouts from the Revolutionary War and owes its expansion to the arrival of the Erie Canal.

Prior to the arrival of settlers, the Seneca Indians inhabited the area. In 1797, they gave up the land following a month long series of heated negotiations called the Treaty of Big Tree. In exchange for this arrangement, the Seneca had the privilege of being confined to reservations and having permission to hunt and fish in the western extent of the territories, surrendering all the land west of the Genesee River.

Three partners from Maryland, among them Nathaniel Rochester, purchased what is now Rochester. Together, the men parceled out building lots and laid out the streets and roads. In 1823, workers completed the final construction connecting the Genesee River to the Erie Canal and the lands east to the Hudson. By the middle of the century, due to its central location, Rochester became the largest flour producer in the nation, earning it the name the *Flour City*. However, as the nation expanded, the wheat industry moved west where the climate was more ideal.

Following the end of the Civil War, Rochester grew to be a technological center, attracting the likes of George Eastman, John Jacob Bausch and Henry Lomb. Eastman, of course, is the founder of Eastman Kodak, while Bausch and Lomb created what became, and remains, one of the world's largest manufacturers and supplier of eye health products.

Cynthia McDonald

Today, Rochester is the third largest city by population in New York State and the home of two of the most recognizable institutions of higher learning in the Tri-State region, the University of Rochester and the Rochester Institute of Technology.

Eastman Kodak

Born in Waterville, New York in 1854, George Eastman is best remembered for his invention of roll film and the accompanying camera, as well as for his extensive philanthropic activities. His father debilitated by illness and no longer able to maintain their farm, moved the family to Rochester when Eastman was six. Home schooled until his later years, following his father's death, Eastman started his own photography business, where he continued to modify the concept of roll film until patenting the product in 1884. Four years later, he came up with the Kodak camera. He founded the Eastman Kodak Company in 1892. The motion picture industry as it is known today would not have been possible without his genius.

His fortune established, Eastman made sizeable donations to both the Mechanics Institute, now called the Rochester Institute of Technology, and MIT. He also endowed the Eastman School of Music at the University of Rochester and funded numerous health and dental institutions.

Although limited by a deteriorating spine, Eastman continued his professional association with Kodak up until the time of his death, concentrating primarily on the company's research efforts. In 1932, frustrated by a pain he could not overcome, he put a gun to his chest and shot himself to death. In the note found at his side, he wrote: My work is done. Why wait?

That brings us to the story of another Rochester resident, and the picture of misanthropy, if ever there was one—Cynthia McDonald.

Cynthia McDonald, a National News Story

The case of Cynthia McDonald made national news. Concerned she had been running a baby farm and that the children were routinely neglected, alerted

71

authorities came to her door at mid-morning and obligated her to permit them entrance. Once inside, they discovered four infants, all of whom described as "mere skeletons".[1] Two, one of whom was a boy by the name of Bobby, were already dead. The surviving two, "their little limbs and arms ... about as large as broom handles"[2] were removed to the Rochester Orphan asylum where nurses provided them with immediate care. Nonetheless, it would be to no avail. They too died.

The attending physician, a Doctor Mulligan, attributed the deaths of all four children to starvation following a thorough medical examination; police declared what little food discovered in the house as unfit for human consumption. Instead of being fed, Mrs. McDonald, to silence their crying and make them sleep, drugged the babies with opium to the point that their digestive systems, even if food was made available, had completely shut down. Detectives later discovered that the two still surviving children, a boy approximately two and one-half years of age and an infant girl were brother and sister. Their mother, Mrs. Hawkins, lived in the house next door.

The coroner's jury found Mrs. McDonald guilty of culpable negligence and jailed her while awaiting trial. Many people believed that she had been farming babies for at least two years prior. Officers investigating the case discovered three children had died that June and suspected the bodies, as well as those of perhaps as many as ten others, had been buried there in the yard.

A blurb appearing in a newspaper out of Kansas, acknowledged that McDonald was but a small part of a much larger problem:

Cynthia McDonald is under arrest in Rochester, New York for starving young children to death in her purported baby farm. It has developed into quite a common practice, in large cities, for parents who desire to get rid of their children to put them in these baby farms when they are slowly starved and dosed to death.[3]

On or about March 9, 1888, according to the Marion Weekly Star, Marion, Ohio, a judge formally sentenced Mrs. McDonald to one year imprisonment and fined her $150. During the process, Mrs. McDonald, described as "about fifty years of age with a shrewd [and] determined face", reportedly sat "calm and manifested not the slightest trace of emotion … as though she had no interest in it."[4]

Victims-4, possibly 10 others

Chapter 11

Rozilla Worcester

History associates Rozilla Worcester with the baby farmers plying their unwholesome services in Manhattan, New York City in the 1870s. However, contrary to the wiles of the trade, Mrs. Worcester came to be investigated due to the fact she seemingly made an effort to comply with the processes required by the city's Health Board. There is some evidence, however, that she only complied in order to cover her deeds of murder.

Many who premeditated the deaths of infants for profit worked at all cost to avoid knowledge of their existence. They would unceremoniously dispose of the lifeless bodies of the babies they murdered by dumping them in swamps, burying them in the yard or paying off the local coroner. Worcester, however, reported the passing of all infants in her charge—the sudden deaths of which were more common at the time—thereby creating the paperwork upon which suspicion of her activities was sown.

It remains unclear, given the contradictory statements of the two sides involved, if Worcester was a murderer or just a poor caregiver.

The Unfortunate Association of Rozilla Worcester

The story of Rozilla Worcester takes place in 1877 in New York City, on the west side of Manhattan. At the time, Mrs. Worcester owned and maintained a

Rozilla Worcester

two-story brick home on Charles Street which many described as "respectable in appearance and the interior ... remarkably neat and clean."[1] Her neighbor, at one time the commander of the Ninth Police Precinct and then of the Twentieth, Captain Washburne, noted she had lived at the address for eleven years and it was common knowledge she provided beds for ladies-in-lying.

On February 6th 1877, Dr. Nagle, Deputy Registrar of Vital Statistics, in his monthly meeting with the Board of Health, noted an inordinate number of infant deaths, six in total, had been associated with Mrs. Worcester's home over the past month. According to the report, the home is described as "one of the dens where abortions are produced and unmarried women are received when they are about to become mothers."[2] The report goes on to add, "Some of the children are sold ... Others are neglected, and when they become burdens are deprived of nourishment and soon die."[3] To support his suspicions, he noted "the diseases from which [the children] died, such as cholera infantum and convulsions, were such as would be produced by neglect or lack of food."[4] Dr. Nagle requested a formal investigation.

The city's Sanitary Superintendent, Walter F. Day, was put in charge of the matter, and he and a Sanitary Inspector by the name of Hughes visited the home. During the interview process, Mrs. Worcester denied the number of deaths and instead acknowledged the deaths of two children within six weeks of each other, one of whom, she stated, was born prematurely and died within minutes of birth. The second child died of marasmus—severe malnutrition due to a lack of carbohydrates and protein. It is assumed the child came to her in that condition. Formal records show both infants received proper and immediate medical care from a physician. In addition, following their passing, formal death certificates were issued and she had copies as evidence. Mr. Day's report countered, stating, "The physicians...who signed...are in good standing...but it appears they made only one visit...two or three days before death."[5]

During the interview, Mrs. Worcester acknowledged she ran a private lying-in hospital, providing beds for both married and single women, but insisting her home served as a place of refuge "for women who had been unfortunate and wished to hide their misfortune from the world."[6] She denied any involvement in "baby farming".

However, if a mother wished not to keep the child, which often was the case, Mrs. Worcester would endeavor to find the babies permanent homes. She stated she placed most infants with married couples who could not have children of their own or who wished to welcome additional children into their homes.

At the time of the visit by the Health Board authorities, only two infants resided in the home. Both were found to be well-fed and healthy. An examination of the public records available at the time showed there had been six reported deaths associated with the property dating back to the previous August. Three of those deaths had been attributed to the excessive heat of the summer. Dr. Evans, of 703 Greenwich Street, verified the three other deaths were attributed to cholera infantum

He had been called to the house to treat the infants. All of the children who died were subsequently issued official burial certificates and presumed properly interred. It was further noted, in the same period of time, women birthed forty babies while in Mrs. Worcester's care.

The Health Board officially decided to "break up [the] place" and, if possible, take "some decided action". Ultimately, they did not charge Mrs. Worcester with any degree of criminal negligence. It is believed she died in 1895 in Brooklyn.

Victims-6 (inconclusive)

All six deaths attributed to a heat wave

Chapter 12

Mrs. Phebe Westlake

Chester is an incorporated village of Orange County, located along the northern border of New Jersey. Native Americans, called the Lenape, first inhabited the area. The earliest explorers brought disease which reduced the Lenape population significantly and as a people, most had disappeared before the arrival of the first European settlers in the 1700s.

In 1740, pioneers established the first settlement in the hamlet of Sugar Loaf. The majority of the inhabitants were local farmers and the craftsmen who served their needs. The Yelverton Inn, built by John Yelverton in 1755 and which served as the center of the village, still stands on Main Street to this day. It counts among its famous guests George Washington, Aaron Burr and Alexander Hamilton.

Orange County is also the location of the United States Military Academy at West Point. Chosen due to its strategic location on the Hudson River, Colonial forces first occupied the garrison in 1778 during the Revolutionary War. The bend in the flow of the river at the point required boats to come to a near standstill to navigate upstream, a strategically poor position for British ships intent on dividing the Colonists.

The Academy was also the impetus for the most infamous traitor in United States history. Benedict Arnold, then serving as a commander of fortifications at West Point, made a deal with the enemy to hand over the fort. In exchange, he would receive both the rank of Brigadier General and a considerable cash payment. Prior to the formal acceptance of terms, he already provided the

British with information concerning colonial forces and strategic locations.

In 1780, Arnold officially switched sides and led a number of battles and attacks against key colonial positions. Prior to Cornwallis' surrender, Arnold gathered his family and returned to England. After, his military and political career stalled and his reputation diminished. Later he returned to North America, settling in New Brunswick where he engaged in various business ventures. He fell ill in 1801 and died later that year.

In 1841, the completion of the Erie Railroad turned Chester into the dairy capital of the region. At its height, local dairy farmers supplied more than 300,000 quarts of milk a day to New York City. The last train pulled out of Chester in 1984 and the tracks were dismantled the year following. The village also originated the Philadelphia Cream Cheese brand, first produced in the late 1800s by William A. Lawrence and which Kraft bought out in 1928. Chester is also recognized for the "Orange Blossoms", a regiment of local volunteers which served with the 124th during the Civil War.

Goshen, New York

Though small in size, Chester is the home or birthplace of a number of significant individuals throughout history. William Terry Jackson was born there in 1794. He served as a U.S. Representative of Congress for the state of New York from 1849-1851. He also served two terms as a Justice of the Peace and as a judge of the court of common pleas.

Hamiltonian, the most famous trotter in history, was foaled on Seely Farm near Sugar Loaf in 1849. His owner, William Rysdyck, is credited with developing the Goshen Race Track into the "Birthplace of the Trotter". To this day, there is a monument, erected in 1893, standing in the middle of the village as a reminder of the combined accomplishments of horse and owner.

As for Phebe Westlake, there is not now, nor will there ever be, any monument.

The Story of Phebe Westlake

Prior to her infamy, little background exists on Phebe Westlake. She was born Phebe Irwin in Ulster County in or about 1813. She married, and around the age of 25 or so, her husband died. Reports indicated his death to be rather sudden and unexpected. At the time of his passing he had on his person a piece of paper—perhaps a small envelope—containing traces of arsenic. The post-mortem examination revealed the poison in his stomach. Yet with no evidence or suspicion of wrong-doing, there was no further investigation and the matter was closed.

Some years later, Phebe arrived in Chester where before long she established the reputation as "industrious ... [skilled in] all manner of woman's work ... [and] professedly pious."[1] She quickly endeared herself to the most well-to-do families in the area and they called upon her whenever they needed her. An 1855 census showed she found employment with the family of Benjamin Johnson as a nanny for the couples' three children.[2] There's no record that she left the family under any dark circumstances, only that she was soon to be otherwise employed.

In Chester, Mr. Pelser and his assistant, Mr. Heard, owned and operated a prominent hotel. The elder Pelser was a widower but had in his home his youngest of two daughters. The older of the two daughters had married a Mr. Clark and at the time resided outside of Chester.

In or around 1853, Mr. Pelser died from erysipelas, an infection of the skin and lymphatic system which results in lesions of the extremities. Left untreated, it can lead to sepsis and death. It is the same disease which took the lives of Queen Anne of Great Britain (1714), Pope Gregory XVI (1846) and baseball player and manager, Miller Huggins (1929).

Upon his passing, the operation of the hotel fell to his daughter. She had most recently been engaged to a wealthy drover from Orange County by the name of Hiram Colwell. They never married.

Due to the rigors of operating the hotel, Mr. Heard recommended to Miss Pelser the hiring of Phebe Westlake to serve as the cook. In a short time after she hired Phebe, Miss Pelser fell ill. Her attending physician could not diagnose her symptoms and ordered her to be confined to bed. To help with the hotel, Mr. Heard summoned the elder sister and husband. Upon their arrival they assumed management so Phebe could assume full responsibility for the care of the younger sister. For all concerned, she presented as genuinely caring and dedicated to the task. Even so, the young lady's condition worsened and she died. Although some people had their suspicions, none suspected Phebe, having witnessed her efforts on behalf of and kindness towards Miss Pelser.

Not long after Miss Pelser's death, Hiram Colwell received a letter signed by the recently deceased, the content of which, among other things, included great praise for Phebe's kindness and asked Mr. Colwell to acknowledge that care. In other words, it suggested Mr. Colwell should reward her financially. However, of most interest to Mr. Colwell and others was the fact that Miss Pelser's illness prevented her from being able to have written the letter herself!

Whether this strange circumstance accounted for Phebe's rather sudden departure is not known as there were no records indicating when exactly Phebe Westlake left the employ of the hotel. Nevertheless, reports state in the fall of 1857, Phebe went to work as the housekeeper for the family of John Bartlett Tuthill, a local merchant, and his wife. They had no children at the time, but Martha Tuthill, known as Little Mary, was expecting and this would be her motive for employing Phebe. Contrary to current practice, in the past, when women were with child, they would often be confined to bed during the final stages prior to the actual birth.

While in the home and attending to her duties, visitors described Phebe as "kind, obliging, assiduous and affectionate."[3] Such warm attention, however, did not spare the soon mother-to-be from a fate similar to that of Miss Pelser.

Soon after Phebe's arrival in the home, Mrs. Tuthill fell ill. Her physician, a Dr. Smith, first diagnosed her with symptoms consistent with those of poisoning. However, he reluctantly conceded that some of these symptoms could also be consistent with pregnancy. Despite his suspicions, and given that he could see no outward evidence of foul play or one who might be suspected, he choose to let the condition run its course. Mrs. Tuthill remained confined to bed. It is believed she died during child birth. Regardless, existing records indicate her baby did not survive.[4]

But the story and Phebe's relationship with Mr. Tuthill does not end there.

Heartbroken and with no desire to remain in his home, John Tuthill left and moved in with his brother, Charles, who was also his business partner. Phebe came along with him and served as both the housekeeper and cook.

A year later, John gave his home over to the care of a Mr. Fuller, a clerk in the Tuthill business. He moved in with his wife. They had no children. As a condition of residence, he had to provide room and board for John. As a result, Phebe found herself without formal employment. However, she did manage to maintain a working relationship with Tuthill and Fuller, bringing them on a daily basis foodstuff and preparing meals.

Perhaps hoping for more permanent employment, one evening less than a week into the arrangements, while preparing and serving dinner, Phebe convinced Mrs. Fuller to join her in a second helping of beans and corn, suggesting if the uneaten portion was left to sit, the food would spoil. Mrs. Fuller agreed. She was unaware, however, that her plate had been poisoned with arsenic. She felt ill that evening and died less than two days later. No one suspected any wrongdoing, nor did anyone suspect poisoning as Phebe had eaten the same meal.

Following the passing of Mrs. Fuller, Phebe returned to work for Charles S. Tuthill and his wife. It is unknown if John also returned to board at this brother's house, but he often joined them for meals. Early in May of 1858, and after Phebe had a confrontational issue with Charles, all three, Charles, his wife and John experienced symptoms similar to those of Mrs. Fuller and Phebe's other victims. They were treated for poisoning and recovered, though Mrs. Tuthill remained ill for an extended period.

The following Monday, Phebe Westlake came down with the same symptoms. The police arrested her soon after on the suspicion of murder. However, she became too ill to be processed and died that Friday.

Aware of the authorities' questions, and hoping to avoid suspicion, Phebe self-administered the poison, believing that if she too evidenced the symptoms, she would be beyond accusation. However, she obviously misjudged the intensity of the dose.

On her death bed, just before she passed, she admitted to the attending pastor, Reverend Wood, that she had sprinkled arsenic on John's toast and on Mrs. Fuller's beans and corn. She did not take responsibility for any of the other murders.

Motives

Although Phebe passed before she could provide a motive for her actions, historians believe she was driven by the attention and appreciation she received from the family members and loved ones of those that she sought to "nurse back to health". Those less empathetic to her, however, are more inclined to believe she took a perverse pleasure in witnessing the slow, suffering deaths of her victims. Given the fatal dose she accidently self-administered, it is reasonable to believe that Phebe did not intend to kill her victims but to keep them ill. The deaths, then, would be more attributable to her lack of sophistication in the administering of the poison than any degree of premeditation.

Arsenic Poisoning

Arsenic is a naturally occurring compound which both free-forms and is found in a number of different minerals. People come in contact with the poison most often through ground water after it leaches through the soil and winds up wells and reservoirs. Called at one time the "King of Poisons" or "inheritance powder", it has been used repeatedly throughout history, taking the lives of Napoleon Bonaparte, Simón Bolívar and Emperor Guangzu of China in 2008.

Identified in the first century by Dioscorides, a Greek physician in Nero's Court, corrupt individuals at the time appreciated it for its physical properties which make it nearly undetectable when added to food or drink. In large doses, it kills rather quickly, the victim, more often than not, dies from shock. In low doses, victims succumb more slowly, which, most conveniently for the perpetrator, allowed for the death to be attributed to something other than poisoning.[5]

In 1836, an English chemist by the name of James Marsh developed a process for detecting arsenic in the human body using a specific chemical test. Treatment of those poisoned involves using chelating agents which separate the metalloid in the blood stream and channel it away from the cells.

As a poison, arsenic works by attacking cellular metabolism. It lowers potassium levels in the blood and stimulates the production of hydrogen peroxide. The result is neurological disturbances, cardio and central nervous system dysfunction, dangerously high blood pressure, anemia, and, death.

Initial symptoms include headache, confusion, and diarrhea, loss of energy, sleepiness and convulsions. As the poison works its way through the system, the victim experiences vomiting, cramping, blood in the stool and urine, hair loss, and the lungs, kidneys and liver begin to shut down.

As for Phebe Westlake, it is not too far-fetched to speculate that she obtained her supply of arsenic in the area and naturally through her own efforts. The proximity of the Greycourt Rock Shelter and the recent draining for farm land of the Chester Meadows swamp, rich in organic material and rock sediment, makes it probable that the compound was present. In addition, as part of her death bed confession, Phebe noted that arsenic had formed on the windowsill of the Tuthill residence, a clear indication she recognized the poison when she saw it.

Victims-4

Chapter 13

Fanny Scofield

Our next story is of Fanny Scofield, a thirteen year old girl that who appeared no different than any other girl from her time and place. The setting is an isolated potato farm in Mexico, New York, towards the end of the 19th century. Many speculate that Fanny's own family, which lived but a couple of miles away, either was unable to support her or believed she was of an age where she could provide for herself in some other fashion. As a result, they sent her to live with a neighboring family to provide care for two infants while the parents tended to their fields. Unfortunately, there occurred a sudden turn of events which no one could have foreseen.

Oswego County, New York 1890s

Mexico is a town situated in north-western New York approximately 10 miles due east from the city of Oswego on the banks of Lake Ontario. Incorporated in 1792, the town is best known for its role in the Underground Railroad, providing temporary sanctuary for slaves seeking their freedom. In 1835, the residents of the town authored and signed a petition asking the country leaders in Washington to abolish slavery and housed an underground station operated by Starr Clark.

The original settlers who arrived during the end of the 18th century found

Fanny Scofield

lands which they described as...

"...gently rolling [with] scarcely a foot of waste land. Excellent drainage is afforded by several streams... The soil is very fertile, and produces large crops of hay, grain and fruit. Strawberries are extensively cultivated."[1]

They also noted the area to be heavily wooded and ideal for lumber, most of which they used for the manufacturing of barrels. However, due to over-harvesting, the settlers quickly used up the natural timber resulting in a majority of sawmills going out of business.

Between 1798 and 1812, following a lessening of the land development restrictions established by Henry Scriba, who held the deed to most of the acreage, and the private construction of a plank road out of Oswego, Mexico experienced an extended period of growth. However, the growth stagnated during the War of 1812, with many fearing for their safety given the village's relatively remote location. From 1812 to 1820, the established population was devastated by the spread of a cholera-like infection which resulted in the deaths of one out of every two people.

Settlers originally established Oswego as a British trading post in 1722. At the time, a small fortification known as Fort Oswego provided the only accommodation. In 1755, the people enlarged the outpost and named it Fort Ontario. That installation, however, became over-run by the French during the Seven Year War and destroyed. The British again rebuilt it in 1759, but did not make use of the fort. During the Revolutionary War, they abandoned it and the American militia burnt it to the ground. The fort then exchanged hands twice more, with an undermanned American garrison facing defeat at the hands of the British in the War of 1812. Later, American troops again occupied it and remained that way until they deemed it no longer a military necessity.

Officials formally designated Oswego as a village in 1828 and a city in 1848. The Erie Canal system reached the village in 1829 and combined with the railroad became a hub for no less than six major railroads and the village became a major port for commerce, manufacturing and business.

Hero

Mary Edwards Walker, the only woman ever to receive the Medal of Honor, and one of only eight civilians, was born in the Town of Oswego in 1832. The youngest of six children, she had only one brother. As a child she worked on her parents' farm. She attended the primary school taught by her mother for her early education. Later, when she was older, she taught at the same school and used the income to attend Geneva Medical College. She graduated in 1855 with a medical degree, the only woman in her class.

Following her graduation, Walker married another doctor and together they established a private practice in Rome, New York. At the time, however, patrons did not respect female doctors or trust their practices and she did not do well.

With the outbreak of the Civil War, Walker volunteered her services as a civilian with the Union Army. As the army did not recognize female doctors, they instead used her as a nurse. Nonetheless, the army required her service as a surgeon once the fighting started, notably in the Battle of Bull Run and the Battle of Fredericksburg.

In 1862 she petitioned the War Department to join the Secret Service to spy on the enemy. The department denied her request. Ironically enough, in 1864, while crossing enemy lines to treat the wounded; the Confederate Army captured her and charged her as a spy. They held Walker as a prisoner of war in Richmond, Virginia. While there she helped a Confederate doctor perform an amputation and afterwards her captors afforded her a less severe confinement. She was later freed as part of a prisoner exchange. President Andrew Johnson presented her with the Medal of Honor in 1865.

In the later part of her life and up until her death in 1919, Walker played a significant role in the Women's Suffragette movement. She focused on the everyday rights of women, which included the right to dress as one pleases. Police arrested her multiple times for wearing what was considered at the time men's clothing. Her trademark, in fact, was the gentleman's top hat she wore while out in public.

Fanny Scofield

Teenage Killer

Fanny Scofield, the daughter of another local farmer, was a thirteen year old girl, described as remarkably attractive,[2] who had been in the employ of the family of Albert and Ella Field since the age of eleven. When initially employed, the Fields had two children. The Fields owned a farm in the village of Mexico, ten miles outside of Oswego. The family employed Fanny to watch the children during the day while the parents worked in their potato fields.

On Sunday, October 31, 1896, the Fields had an early breakfast at the crack of dawn, after which they went together out into the farmland for the day's work. Their daughter, Fern, 2 years old, who had been put to bed following the prior evening's supper, was still asleep. She had been in fine health at the time and, besides a relatively harmless fall upon the stairs a day or two prior, had not been ill any time recently. Her parents left Fanny in charge.

Mr. Fields returned to the house sometime around 3:30 in the afternoon to retrieve a horse and wagon from the barn while his wife remained out in the fields. While Mr. Fields was out by the barn, Fern came out of the house to walk beside him. Before they had gone but a short distance, the little girl told her father she did not feel well. He told her to go back to the house. Within a step or two, she started to vomit and did so multiple times. The father, noticing the appearance of grey matter in the vomit, picked-up his daughter in his arms and brought her back to the house. He then hurried to retrieve his wife.

Back in the house with her mother, Fern complained of stomach pains and continued to vomit. They placed her in a warm tub while Mr. Fields went into the village to obtain medication. The medication failed to alleviate the symptoms, which by this time included convulsions. The family summoned their local physician.

It was almost 9:00 at night by the time Dr. Huntington arrived. When he first examined the little girl, he found her non-responsive, in a cold sweat and with no discernible pulse. He gave her brandy and tried ammonia, but failed to revive her. She died soon afterwards. However, Dr. Huntington also noted the grey powdery matter in her vomit and collected a sample to analyze.

The following day, Dr. Huntington sent the sample of vomit to the coroner, a man by the name of Vowinkle. He immediately forwarded it to Dr. William Manlius Smith of Syracuse, a chemist. He found the presence of arsenic in sufficient enough quantity to cause both convulsions and death. Armed with the information, Coroner Vowinkle initiated a formal inquest and a coroner's jury was formed.

Immediate suspicion fell on Fanny, the only other person in proximity to the little girl. Vowinkle interviewed the teen and discovered that upon waking from her nap, Fern told Fanny that she was hungry. Two versions of what happened next emerged. Fanny either gave her a glass of milk, or more likely, she gave the girl the remainder of the beef broth which the Fields had eaten earlier in the day. Try as he might, however, the coroner was unsuccessful in eliciting any further information from the teen girl; she denied any knowledge as to how the child would have come to be poisoned.

Through further investigation, Vowinkle discovered a poison known as *Rough on Rats*, containing arsenic, present in no less than six locations throughout the house. Mrs. Fields had sprinkled it on Johnny Cakes, a sort of cornmeal flatbread favored at the time, and placed the bait in small dishes on the sills and cabinet tops—all out of the reach of the child—to attract and kill rodents in and around the house. Fanny claimed to have burned the Johnny Cakes.

Further conversations with Mrs. Fields revealed that Fanny knew of the *Rough on Rats* and had at one time been asked to store the container out of reach. She later saw Fanny with a small bottle or glass vial that contained a white powder. When asked by Mrs. Fields as to its content, Fanny claimed she did not know.

During the days following Fern's death, a number of local people came forward to report their suspicions concerning Fanny. Mrs. Marilla Rose, who lived in Texas, seven miles from the Fields farm, told of arriving at the home when summoned to help with Fern. The child yet lived when she arrived and it was Fanny who told her about the sickness. The next morning, Fanny approached Mrs. Rose at the local well and asked her how she thought Fern would have been exposed to the arsenic. Fanny said it would be best if a formal examination were not to be undertaken, as confirmation of the poisoning would only cause the family further anguish. She also, stated she wished she had the opportunity to wash the basin into which Fern vomited, a statement of which Mrs. Rose immediately became suspicious.

A second neighbor, Miss Grace Spoor, testified at the coroner's inquest that upon hearing the coroner may find some other cause than poisoning for the death, Fanny appeared visibly relieved.

A third neighbor, Miss Ella A. Carlton, confirmed much of which the other two ladies had reported, and added that in her opinion, Fanny seemed happy with the death of the child. When informed that death by poisoning had been confirmed, she stated without being asked that it was not she who did it.

As an additional result of the inquest, authorities discovered that the Field's other child; a girl of 13 months, died of similar circumstances the previous July, but at the time was thought to have passed from natural causes. Only after the death of Fern, did the Fields recall the similarities of the two deaths, including the presence of the grayish powder.

Police arrested Fanny on November 13, 1896 under the suspicion of murdering the two Fields children. They initially took her by car to the county jail at Oswego, Fanny's first time ever in an automobile, which caused her to ask many questions about the experience and without indicating any awareness of the gravity of her predicament. Ultimately, due to her age, officials made arrangements for her to stay with the family of the sheriff.[3]

As for Fanny's fate, there is brief mention of a formal hearing in a court in Mexico, New York, but that the proceeding adjourned without a decision. In all likelihood, given Fanny's age and a decidedly different societal attitude, legally speaking, in terms of the unnatural death of a child, Scofield may have been remanded to a local orphanage or other juvenile institution until she came of age, at which time she would have rejoined society.

Victims-2

AVENGERS

Chapter 14
Roxanna Druse

The tale of Roxanna Druse is not one of serial killings—only a single husband perished—but is included due to its historical significance in New York State. Of course, the horrific nature of the crime and the threat that Mrs. Druse posed to her two children and a nephew add both to the interest of the plot and the cold brutality of the antagonist.

Herkimer County, New York 1880s

Herkimer is in north-central New York, with Cooperstown and Oneonta to the south and Syracuse to the west. Albany is to the east. The town of Warren is on the southern border of the county and east of Richfield Springs.

Prior to being inhabited by German settlers in 1708, the lands that make up the current Village of Herkimer and the surrounding county belonged to the Mohawks of the Iroquois Nation. The heavily wooded lands made travel difficult. By 1722, the population had expanded and continued to do so until the French and Indian War. At the time, many referred to the area as the German Flatts. Up until that point, the lands alongside the Mohawk River had been divided into 30 acre lots with a total of almost 100 homesteads using the acreage to farm. The settlers built Fort Herkimer on the south side of the river.

In 1758, with the onset of the French and Indian War, a company of French and Indian soldiers attacked the homesteads on the south side of the river without warning or provocation and slaughtered. Captain Nicholas Herkimer managed to get the survivors inside the fort walls and preserve the settlement. Later they built a second fort, Fort Dayton, on the north side of the river.

Again Herkimer served a prominent role in the Revolutionary war. Captain Herkimer assembled his militia at the fort and marched on the British fortification in Oriskany, twenty miles to the west. Although he suffered serious wounds at the onset of the battle, his forces managed to significantly weaken the British effort by preventing the joining of British troops with the Tory and Indian forces they expected. Within days, General Benedict Arnold marched on Oriskany from Fort Dayton with 1200 men, only to find that the British had fled. The battle is considered the turning point of the war.

By the beginning of the 19th century, Fort Herkimer became a hub for the stage coaches traveling from eastern New York to the west. As a center point, the coaches often stopped to rest their horses and replenish their supplies. With the arrival of the Erie Canal in 1825 and the construction of the Herkimer Hydraulic Canal eight years later, the village transformed into an industrial center, including potash production, tanneries and whiskey distilleries. The Village of Herkimer was formally incorporated in 1807, with various amendments to the charter up until 1875, when it became the village it is today.

Historical Reference

In an article that appeared in the *Alton Evening Telegraph* in 1886, an Illinois newspaper, the journalist, in response to the number of petitions sent by women to Governor Hill to appeal the sentence of Roxanna Druse, stated, "The petition leads one to the conclusion that the ladies don't want equal rights so much as they claim."[1]

The Story of Roxanna Druse

Roxanna Druse was born Roxalana Teftt, either in 1846 or 1847, and not too far from Warren in Herkimer County. Both of her parents died when she was about 10 years of age and left her to fend for herself. For the most part, she found shelter with local families for which she provided help around the house. She often picked hops at harvest time. During one such harvest she met her future husband, William Druse.

Although at the time of her trial, records described her as "a frail, little woman of about forty years, who, from appearance would not hurt a dove,"[2] William took a fancy to her then thin and girlish figure. They married in 1863. Born in 1828, he was far older than she. He also held a reputation for being shiftless and worthless, as well as somewhat daft and with an ungovernable temper.[3] Together they settled in on his farm, a 60 acre piece of property he inherited from his father.

As might have been predicted, the relationship didn't work out well. Roxanna suffered both physical and verbal abuse from Druse, and he treated his three children in much the same manner. One of the children, Nellie, died at the age of ten. Most people were aware that at one time he choked Roxanna until she passed out, another time he beat her with a horse whip and he slapped and cuffed her around on a daily basis. While in prison, she acknowledged she hadn't slept with him in twelve years.

According to available records, on the day of the murder, December 18, 1884, William Druse awakened and went from the second floor of their home where he slept down to the first floor to start a fire in the hearth. As it was December, it is safe to assume it was fairly cold outdoors. Four other family members resided in the house at the time. The first boy, George (or William) was either age 10 or 11 and the natural son of Roxanna and William. The second boy Frank Gates, a 13 year old nephew residing with the family, slept upstairs with his cousin. Roxanna and her 19 year-old daughter, Mary, slept down in the parlor.

After starting the fire to warm the house, William went out to the barn to begin his daily chores. The women of the house arose soon after and prepared breakfast. The boys then joined them to eat. Following the meal, Roxanna sent the boys out to the yard but told them to remain close by as she might need them.

Sometime later, William returned to the house and he and Roxanna started to argue about some grocery bills that had not been paid. Such arguing was commonplace and well-known to the neighbors.

From this point on, the argument can be made that Roxanna had anticipated the confrontation with her husband; perhaps she may even have strategically initiated it. She walked away from him and went into the pantry. She came out with an apron beneath which she hid a .22 caliber revolver. The gun, from what she claimed later as she prepared to go to the gallows, was given to her by Charles Gates, who showed her how to use it.

Meanwhile, Mary had secured a length of rope and at a signal from her mother, threw it around the torso and arms of her then seated father. Roxanna ran up to him, put the revolver inches from him and fired. The bullet struck him in the neck. He fell from the chair and to the floor. Unable to make the gun fire a second time, she summoned the two boys into the house and handed the revolver to Frank. She ordered him to fire a second shot, saying if he refused, she would shoot him. He complied and fired. Both bullets found their mark, but William, owing to the somewhat small ammo, yet survived.

Still confined by the rope and incapacitated by the three wounds, he lay on the floor, injured but alive. Roxanna went for an axe which her husband had borrowed from a neighbor. Understanding what would happen next, William used his last breaths to beg for his life. Roxanna, however, was beyond compassion and delivered a single blow to his head. Not yet satisfied, she swung again and again until she managed to fully decapitate him. She then retrieved the head from the floor, wrapped it in her apron and placed it into a sack of buckwheat. Charles Gates later discarded it near Richfield Springs.

The story, however, does not end there. With the help of her daughter and a gentleman who lived nearby (presumed to be Gates),[4] the three proceed to use the axe and a large kitchen knife to dismember the body. While they worked at their ghastly task, they sent the two boys to fetch wood. The group started roaring fires in both the kitchen stove and the fireplace and they set large pots of water to boil. Though it took all the day and part of the evening, Roxanna and Mary managed to reduce William's remains to ashes. Some rumors abounded that parts of the body had been fed to the hogs, but Roxanna went to the gallows denying the gossip. They disposed of the ashes in a pond within proximity to the property, along with the murder weapons. Roxanna then threatened the boys, saying that they too would be killed if they spoke to anyone of the incident.

Unbeknownst to Roxanna, as she **burned** the remains, a thick yellow smoke with an unsettling aroma billowed from the chimneys and attracted the attention of a passerby. He noted too that the windows of the door and the front of the house had been covered with newspaper.

Confronted two days later with the absence of her husband, whom the community well regarded despite his reputation, Roxanna explained he was off on one of his jaunts, having gone to New York to obtain a patent on a mechanism he had been developing. It wasn't until more than a month later, suspicion finally exceeding the extent of her efforts to the contrary, that police launched an official investigation. The murder came to light when Frank, the nephew, who many believed to be mentally handicapped, told his father of the event and then later confessed to some neighbors who pressed him on the issue. Officers arrested all four suspects in late May of 1885.

The Trial and Sentencing

Following leads obtained by talking to the two boys, the local authorities recovered the ashes of Williams remains from the stove in the house and the weapons thrown into the pond. Faced with overwhelming evidence, Roxanna's defense lawyer, H. D. Luce, had no choice but to argue self-defense, suggesting that after years of verbal abuse and threats from her husband, and fearing for the safety of her children and herself, she saw no choice but to act first. Given the brutal details of the murder, the jury could not be sympathetic to Roxanna's plight. After deliberating for less than two hours, and this after 15 days of trial, they returned a verdict of guilty. On October 6, 1885, in the courtroom in Little Lakes, Herkimer County, the judge sentenced Roxanna to hang by the neck until dead.

Just about two weeks before her scheduled hanging, November 25, 1885, the defense team made an appeal. The court denied the appeal and set a new date for her hanging for December 29th of the following year, 1886. The sentence was again appealed and again her hanging delayed. In February of 1887, Governor Hill upheld the sentence. There would be no further appeal.

On the day of her reckoning—almost three full years following her husband's murder—an armed militia escorted Roxanna Druse to the gallows, in order to keep the gathering mob from carrying out a lynching of their own.[5]

According to witnesses, it wasn't until she was upon the stairs and climbing that her icy demeanor suddenly thawed and she shed tears. By then it was too late. Immediately upon reaching the platform, the executioner placed the hood over her head and followed it with the noose.

At that time in the state's history, the preferred gallows did not favor the trap door design and instead relied on a counter weight which would spring the condemned off their feet and upward where the force of momentum combined with the body's weight would break the neck. In the case of Roxanna Druse, the device malfunctioned. Her frame was too small for the mechanism to be effective and instead she hung in air until she finally strangled, her legs kicking and twitching and horrible noises issuing from beneath the hood until death finally came fifteen minutes later. She was the first woman to be executed in Herkimer County in the previous forty years. Due to the incompetence of the procedure, the State of New York adopted death by electrocution.

As for the children, officials released the two boys due to a lack of evidence and the extenuating circumstances. Despite her mother's signed confession that she acted alone, Mary, however, was committed to the state penitentiary at Syracuse for life.

To add some final interest to the story, there are those who swear that the ghost of Roxanna returned, as she promised, to haunt the jail cell in which she thought herself unjustly held. Moans and murmurs of despair, never before experienced, routinely manifested themselves from out of the emptiness and were reminiscent of the sounds she made while swinging at the end of her rope.[6]

Her body was laid to rest in a vault in Oak Hill Cemetery.

Victims-Only 1

Chapter 15
Mary Antone

Much like the case of Roxanna Druse, Mary Antone could not be labeled a serial killer. Her story is included due to its singularity and place in history. Mary was the first Native American woman tried and executed in a court of law in the state of New York.

Madison County, New York 1810s

Going back to the 17th century, Madison County was originally part of Albany County which included territories now in part of the state of Vermont and, technically, it had no limiting boundaries extending to the Pacific coast. Prior to the arrival of colonial settlers, all the land around Lake Oneida belonged to Native Americans as part of the Iroquois Nation. These peoples included the Oneida, the Onondaga, the Seneca, the Cayuga and the Mohawk.

In the 18th century, the English laid claim to most of the land and then divided it into two counties, Cumberland and Gloucester. Loyalists settled Tryon County in 1772. However, sensing the impending conflict between the British and the Colonists, and feeling exposed and unprotected in a land very much a wilderness, most of the Loyalists fled north to Canada.

Following the Revolutionary War, locals changed the county name to honor General Richard Montgomery and it became Montgomery County. In appreciation for their efforts on the part of the Colonists, officials gave the Oneida Indians a significant extent of land around the lake as a reservation. However, Colonists drove those Iroquois tribes loyal to the British from their lands, largely as the result of Sullivan's Raid. With their villages and crops destroyed, those that chose not to migrate north to Canada were exposed to the winter elements and eventually starved to death.

In 1788, the Clinton Purchase, later declared unconstitutional by the United States Government, managed to manipulate the Oneida into surrendering a large part of their southern land holdings, which they then sold to new settlers. In 1802, they again agreed to give-up another 20,000 acres so that the Lenape would have a place to call home.

In 1789, Ontario County separated from Montgomery County thereby reducing its size. Two years later, the counties of Herkimer, Tioga and Otsego also split from Montgomery. In 1798, Herkimer and Tioga joined to form Chenango County, and in 1806, Chenango became Madison.

Peterboro is a small town in Smithfield in Madison County. Its first settlers began development in 1795. The town gets its name from Peter Smith who arrived with his family in 1806. Smith was a partner of John Jacob Astor. Using the wealth that he too accumulated in the fur trade, he financed and held most of the business and property interests in the surrounding area.

After his passing, his son Gerritt inherited his father's holdings, which he continued to manage and grow. The younger Smith was a known advocate of abolition and many believe his estate was have been used by Harriet Tubman herself as part of the Underground Railroad, as well as a place of refuge for John Brown and Frederick Douglass.

Smith also held membership in the Secret Six, a group of men who secretly funded the 1859 raid on Harper's Ferry by the abolitionist John Brown. Brown believed the abolishment of slavery could only happen through armed insurrection. The raid ended unsuccessfully. U.S. militia captured Brown, convicted him and sentenced him to die by hanging.

The Gerritt Smith Estate, which still stands today, was declared a National Landmark in 2001.

Mary Antone

Women's Rights and Abolitionists

Elizabeth Cady Stanton, a leading figure in the early women's rights movement, an abolitionist and a cousin of Gerritt Smith, was born in Johnstown in 1815. Cady Stanton lead the composition of the Declaration of Rights and Sentiments, a sort of women's Declaration of Independence, which she presented at the first ever women's rights convention organized by women. It took place in Seneca Falls, New York in 1848. At the time, some described the document as, "the most shocking and unnatural event ever recorded in the history of womanity."[1]

In 1851, Cady Stanton met Susan B. Anthony and the two joined efforts in the Temperance Movement, which most saw as closely linked to women's rights. As Anthony had no children or husband, Cady Stanton left most of the traveling and speaking engagements to her, and instead, dedicated herself to the writing of Anthony's material.

Later, as the women's rights movement grew and splintered, Cady Stanton and Anthony lobbied against the proposed 14th and 15th Amendments, arguing that the language was not significantly inclusive of the concerns of women—primarily the right to vote—and that those concerns should be considered separate from that of Black men. Many people considered Cady Stanton's rhetoric racist.

In 1870, Congress passed the Fifteenth Amendment, and while it gave Black men the right to vote, it did not extend the same right to women, who were already believed to be adequately represented by their husband's vote. Despite the intent of the Amendment, both Cady Stanton and Anthony presented themselves at the voting poll and demanded the right to cast their votes. Officials at the polls denied their requests.

Cady Stanton dedicated the latter part of her life to writing. Her most well-known works are *The Women's Bible*, 1895 and 1898, and *The Solitude of Self*, 1892. She passed away on October 6, 1902. The U.S. Secretary of the Interior declared her home in Seneca Falls as a National Historic Landmark in 1965.

The Tale of Mary Antone (Antoine)

Mary Antone, born in 1794, belonged to the Oneida tribe living in the area of Madison County, New York. Sometime prior to her hanging on September 13, 1814, a local landowner, John Jacobs, witnessed her killing another Native Indian girl from a different tribe. She did so by stabbing her multiple times with a knife. Jealousy had motivated her. Apparently, a male love interest recently rejected her advances and he then took up with the victim.

Following a statement made by Jacobs to the local authorities, police arrested and charged Antone with murder. They tried her in Smithfield and found her guilty. The court sentenced her to the gallows. Her tribe vigorously denounced the proceedings, taking the stance that the white man's court had no jurisdiction over Indian matters, especially when the issue did not involve anyone outside the tribe.

A few days prior to the sentencing, Antone's father, Abram, and a brother came into Smithfield adorned as if prepared for battle. In response, a Captain Daniel Petrie, commander of the local militia, had his men take up arms and stand at the ready. However, neither side took any action.

Further reports state that while crews constructed the gallows but a few yards from the grist mill and the creek, Abram could be seen up on the ridge overlooking the spot, pacing back and forth as if contemplating a means by which to rescue his daughter.

On the day of the hanging, a large number of tribal members made their way into the village early in the morning and milled about the streets and a local store, as if establishing position. Captain Petrie, who just happened to be the store owner and had a good command of the Native language, cautioned the arrivals against doing anything rash, and for good measure, commanded some of his men to stand on guard.

When the time came to carry out the sentence, Sheriff Pratt escorted Mary Antone to the gallows. As he did so, Abram was allegedly heard to say, "Me kill him!"[2] The threat could not be taken lightly. Many believed Mr. Atone had killed two other men and a child. The first, a man from Canada, who had referred to him as an Indian dog, he followed for a number of days until locating him at a roadside inn. That evening, he snuck up on the man while he was sleeping and plunged a knife into his chest. A fellow Indian became his second victim who he believed had deceived him concerning money. He killed the child because it would not stop crying.

Despite the alleged threat, both Sheriff and prisoner proceed to the gallows unmolested. Once in position, the executioner gave Abram permission to climb the scaffold and say a final good-bye to his daughter. He did so stoically, taking her by the hand and without exchange of words. He then climbed down the way he went up, and without looking back walked away. The sentence was then carried out.

As for John Jacobs, the witness to the murder, Abram Antone swore vengeance, holding him responsible for his daughter's death. Jacobs, fearing for his life, kept a low profile and his distance from Madison County. Sometime later Abram himself sent John word that all was forgiven and he had no further reason to fear.

Jacobs took the man at his word and returned. Shortly thereafter, while working in his fields, he saw the figure of Abram approaching him in a manner suggestive of friendship. Once in arm's length, Abram extended his hand as if to offer it in reconciliation. As Jacob acted in like manner, the vengeful father produced a knife and stabbed him in the heart.

At age 73, and almost nine years to the day his daughter met her fate as the first recorded female ever hung in New York State, Abram Antone died on those same gallows, tried and convicted for the murder of John Jacobs.

Victim-Only 1,

Lover's girlfriend

Father was serial killer with at least 3 victims

Question of Sanity

Chapter 16
Ella Holdridge

The tale of Ella Holdridge differs from the stories of our other women killers primarily due to her age. She was only fourteen at the time. But there is also sadness to it, as she obviously suffered from an emotional dysfunction that prohibited her from distinguishing between fantasy and reality, and which, inarguably, accounted for her inability to appreciate the finality of death. She did not find motivation in hate or anger, but by a sense of beauty that most would find to be incongruent with what one would consider a rational perspective.

Erie County, New York 1890s

Tonawanda is a city on the east banks of the Niagara River in Erie County in western New York. It is south of the Erie Canal and north of Buffalo.

Henry Anguish arrived in 1808 and is the first known settler in the area. He built himself a log cabin. By 1811, the population of the area swelled enough that he added a tavern. In 1825, the Erie Canal made its way into the hamlet and the area began to grow. The town was formally incorporated in 1836. Thanks to access provided by the canal and the subsequent arrival of the railroad, Tonawanda became a key provider of lumber to the surrounding area.

In 1892, Tonawanda made national news when the foreman of the Weston lumber yards, which employed non-union workers, after being struck on the head by a stone, pulled out a revolver and began firing into a crowd of some 500 striking union laborers who rallied to prevent the non-union lumbermen from working. Eight policemen joined him and also fired upon the crowd. Apparently, some among the striking workers were also armed, and they returned gun fire. Reports stated that several men were struck, including two policemen. One officer, by the name of Kingsley, was struck in the stomach and later died as a result.

The striking workers moved on to South Tonawanda, the location of another lumber mill. Town officials took measures to quell the rioting workers, including dispersing armed policemen throughout the town. The issue went unresolved for most of the year.

Also in the same year, railroad workers went on a strike which momentarily brought all freight movement through the area to a halt. Non-union workers replaced the striking workers which resulted in violent clashes designed to keep the trains from rolling. The Governor responded by calling up Militia from various parts of the state, most of whom had been stationed outside the city in the Cheektowaga rail yards. More than 14 different regiments and over 700 soldiers were on hand. Immediately following their arrival, the union workers ambushed the 13th and 23rd from the Brooklyn Militia while they guarding the trestles belonging to the Delaware and Lackawanna rail company. The striking workers eventually dispersed and rail operations resumed as close as possible to normal using replacement switchmen. This disruption also lasted a good part of the year.

In 1904, Tonawanda separated itself from what became North Tonawanda and was designated a city.

Sainthood

Father Nelson Baker, best known for his founding of the City of Charity, was born in Buffalo in 1841. Following his service in the Civil War, where he served as part of the militia that quelled the draft riots of 1863, he returned to Buffalo and began his career as an ordained priest. The diocese assigned him first to work alongside Father Hines at Limestone Hill, then an orphanage for boys, located in Tonawanda. He later became the superintendent of the institution, but resigned after only a year due to financial troubles which he believed could not be resolved. He transferred to another parish, but at the behest of the Bishop returned and took over complete management of Limestone Hill.

To raise the necessary funds leading to solvency, Father Baker turned not to local business, but instead to the more well-to-do ladies in the surrounding parishes. Writing 1000s of letters by hand, he convinced his eventual supporters to donate twenty-five cents each, all of which he assured them would go the cause. The overwhelming response resulted in the creation of the Association of Our Lady of Victory, the first piece in his City of Charity.

Over the next 25 years, Baker, with the aid of his supporters, opened Limestone Hill to children from every state in the Union and Canada, tripling the number of orphans served, established the Working Home for Boys, the Our Lady of Victory Infant Home for young and unwed mothers, a maternity and general hospital under the Our Lady of Victory name and a European-style basilica, also named Our Lady of Victory. Baker died in 1936 of natural causes. He was 95 years of age. The Vatican named him a "Servant of God" in 1987, and in 2011, Pope Benedict XVI moved him towards canonization, declaring him "Venerable Nelson Baker".

John Neumann, the first Bishop from the Tonawanda parish, was born John Nepomucene Neumann in 1811 in Bohemia, part of the Austrian Empire. He came to the United States in 1836. He was ordained in St. Patrick's Cathedral in New York City. Church officials assigned him to the Niagara Falls area where most settlers had emigrated from Germany. He tended to all the lands between Lake Ontario down to Pennsylvania.

Required to travel the countryside on horse, Neumann took up residence in North Bush, which is now a part of Tonawanda. He served as the pastor of the St. John the Baptist Church, from where he conducted his missionary work.

In 1840, longing for a greater sense of community, he requested a transfer from Tonawanda. The church granted his request. They first reassigned him to Pittsburgh and after to parishes in Maryland. In 1852, coinciding with a heavy influx of Europeans, Neumann was appointed Bishop of Philadelphia. Under his leadership, the diocese grew exponentially, building new churches at the rate of one a month. In addition, he established the city's first parochial school system, increasing the number of schools from one to 200—in less than eight years. Neumann suffered a stroke and died in January of 1860. He was 48 years of age.

Pope Paul VI canonized Neumann in 1977. His remains lie interred beneath the altar at The National Shrine of Saint John Neumann at the Parish of St. Peter the Apostle in Philadelphia.

Thrill Killer

At fourteen years old, Ella Holdridge lived in Tonawanda, Buffalo, New York. On July 19, 1892, police took her into informal custody for the premeditated murder of a seven year-old girl by the name of Louisa Stermer, the daughter of Mrs. Herman Stermer.

As the story goes, Ella had an obsession with funerals and would attend as many of the local wakes and burials as possible, invited or not. Once there, she would place herself as close as possible to the open casket or the burial plot to gain an unobstructed view of the deceased. Afterwards she would return home and tell her mother of everything she saw.

Little Louisa Stermer fell ill on July 7th. The family summoned the local doctor, a Dr. Harris, and he attributed her ailment, with symptoms similar to cholera morbus, "to summer complaint and treated [her] accordingly."[1] Despite the doctor's efforts, the child, without gaining consciousness, died two days later.

Of course, Ella appeared at Louisa's services, and one witness described her as "solemn and quiet, her eyes flashing with excitement and her cheeks rosy red."[2]

The following Wednesday, a neighbor woman by the name of Eggleston had to be away for the day and left her two young daughters, Susie, age 10, and Jennie, age 5, home unattended. Ella paid the home a visit and promised to make the girls a treat. She made them hot cocoa into which she put rat poison. When one of the girls noted that the concoction tasted funny, she pushed the child down on the couch and forced the liquid into her mouth. She promised both girls they would be alright and made them swear they would not tell their mother of the incident. Both girls became seriously ill and when their mother discovered them she called a Dr. Edmonds. Although there is no official report of what became of the two girls, the local journalist covering the story indicated a lack of confidence that either would survive.[3]

Either that same day or the one to follow, Ella managed a third victim, a five year old boy by the name of George Garlock. She poisoned him too when she convinced him to eat some food she had prepared. Dr. Edmonds also treated him.

Suspecting that Ella may be behind the sudden rash of misfortune befalling the local children, the doctor had her brought to him. He confronted her with his suspicions and she rather matter-of-factly admitted her role. When asked as to her motive for endangering the Eggleston children, she stated that "she wanted to go to their funeral because they would look so nice dead."[4]

Police immediately suspected that Ella might have been responsible for the death of Louisa Stermer. When asked, she said, "Yes, she looked awfully pretty in a coffin."[5]

When interviewed, Ella's mother recalled her daughter seemed quite excited by Louisa's illness, running back and forth from the girl's house to her own home to keep her mother informed on her progress. She first told her mother that she thought Louisa was going to go to heaven; then, most joyously, that she was almost dead; and finally, jumping up and down and clapping her hands with glee, she must have died because everyone was crying and a man showed up at the house with a box.

Asked how she knew the poison, known as *Rough on Rats*, would kill the children, she answered, and "If it killed rats and mice it would kill children."[6]

It came to light after the fact that Ella held responsibility for the poisoning of three other children who lived under the care of Father Nelson Henry Baker at his institution at Limestone Hill, a home for orphans. However, when confronted, she told the Father that she had given the children hot water to drink. As the children did not experience any serious after effects, the matter was given no special attention.

Local officials remanded Ella to the care of Father Baker after taking her into custody and kept her at Limestone Hill for safekeeping until it could be decided what to do with her.

Historical Note

Following the Civil War, a group of benevolent individuals, adamant that if left untreated, the youth problems of the time would threaten the moral fabric of society, initiated the Child-Saving Movement. Their efforts brought about significant changes to the Juvenile Justice System in the United States, especially in large urban areas such as Philadelphia and New York.

By the time of Ella Holdridge's arrest, juveniles could no longer be treated in the same way as adults. Recent reform allowed for juveniles to be processed before separate courts and viewed as youthful offenders and not criminals. They considered their actions in terms of their immaturity and a lack of understanding as to the consequences, and therefore they could not be held to the same level of accountability as adults. The objective of the Justice System moved from punishment to treatment and the development of productive citizens.[7]

So despite the cold, calculated nature of Ella's criminal behavior, she likely would not have been found guilty of murder or have been punished with any lengthy prison sentence. In all probability, she remained a ward of the Limestone Hill Institution until the age of 16 or 17, after which they permitted her to go on her way.

Victims-possibly as many as 5

Chapter 17

Mary Runkle

In late August of 1847, a man by the name of Runkle was found dead in his home on West Street. His wife, Mary, summoned a doctor to their home. During the visit, the doctor could see that someone attempted to remove blood stains from the floor. Runkle himself was found to be bruised about the head and neck—clear bruises indicated he had been choked—and he was missing three teeth, which they discovered in the room. In addition, the doctor found bruises on his hips, elbows and knees.

When asked to provide an explanation for the man's condition, Mrs. Runkle explained that her old and feeble husband "had taken with a fit, got out of bed, and fell down on the floor two or three times."[1] Showing bruises that she herself sported, she claimed her husband's thrashing body battered her as she tried to lift the man back to the bed. The physician doubted her story.

An investigation by police uncovered bloodied clothing belonging to both Mr. and Mrs. Runkle, and to their 12 year-old daughter, who may have witnessed and participated in the beating death of the older gentleman. Officers discovered the clothes bundled together and hidden in another part of the house.

Prior to relocating to the home on West Street, the Runkles lived in Westmoreland in Montgomery County. From reports provided by their neighbors, they held an unhappy union. Nearby residents often heard the couple engaged in loud and angry arguments. In addition, their departure from Westmoreland may have been hastened by larceny charges brought against them for stealing clothes from their neighbors.

Further, while living in Montgomery County, the Runkles, who apparently were well-enough connected, became suspects in the disappearance of a traveling peddler and the deaths of their two younger children, both of whom drowned "by the agency of some person or persons unknown."[2]

Ultimately, prosecutors tried Mary Runkle found her guilty of the murder of her husband. It is alleged she confessed her crime to a Dr. Smith and an undersheriff by the name of Eames; however, there is no indication that she admitted involvement in the other murders of which she was suspected. Mary's lawyer made an unsuccessful appeal for commutation of the sentence to the then Governor Young. He based his denial on "the ground of the clearness of the evidence and the aggravated character of the murder."[3]

On the day of her execution, on or about November 20, 1847, Runkle "lay almost motionless on her bed, her eyes half closed, and her right hand resting … on her bosom … as if she was engaged in deep and unhappy thought. She spoke only in whispers … [saying,] she was prepared for death having made peace with her Maker."[4] The authorities came for her just before noon. They escorted Mary to the gallows in the jail in Whitesboro and placed her on a chair beneath the hanging noose. She and the jailor shared a final prayer, Runkle's head rested upon his shoulder. The executioner bound her arms to the chair, and she reportedly showed no emotion. Moments later, a bell rang, the floor opened up and the chair fell. Without a sound, her chest heaving only slightly, Runkle hung suspended for twenty minutes. Once pronounced dead, the executioner removed her from the rope and laid her within a plain coffin. Her body was turned over to friends.

Victims-possibly 3

Conclusion

When we research deeper into the lives of the women profiled in this book, it is clear that categorizing any particular one of them as either a Black Widow, Angel of Death, Baby Farmer, Avenger or insane falls short of understanding not only the complexity of their individual motivation, but the physical and social environment in which they lived.

In the each of these cases, with the exception of the two teenagers, the argument can be made that the key motivating factor behind their murderous activity was survival. By survival, we suggest the most primitive level: the fear of being without food, clothing and shelter; the fear of being alone in a hostile world. Couple this anxiety with below level intelligence—few of these women possessed any education and many could be described in terms suggesting some degree of disability, general ignorance, isolated environments, weak and non-supportive husbands and lack of opportunity— and you hold the perfect recipe for the stew of their actions.

Physical Environment

A majority of these women lived in relative isolation and anonymity, either in rural areas in which people resided far from each other or nestled in some indistinct residence on an urban street. Removed from one's nearest neighbor or left undetected among the masses, each was provided the ideal setting for committing murder. For a number of the ladies, McCraney and Halliday, to name two, the vast and unsettled lands between one town or city and the next, coupled with primitive means of transportation, allowed them a physical distance from previous incidents and they could settle elsewhere in silence. Their new neighbors, none the wiser, allowed them to remain above suspicion while second and third husbands, otherwise healthy, without warning died from mysterious maladies.

The science of the time, and especially in terms of doctors serving as general practitioners, lacked modern advancements so the subtle applications of poisons such as arsenic, and the resultant symptoms, were readily assumed to be common childhood maladies or those associated with age and exposure. Add, then, reasonable doubt—the perceived demureness and physical inferiority of a woman, for example—and you have enough to look beyond the obvious truth.

These crimes also occurred at point in history when pharmaceuticals and opiates—now regulated by many stringent laws—could be obtained and found both readily available and cheap. Catherine Claus, who, as evidenced by living in a swamp and wearing rags as clothing, had very little money, nonetheless, obtained opium with ease and in no small quantity. Cynthia McDonald, no better off financially, came to possess both opium and laudanum, and in quantities sufficient to drug multiple infants into unconsciousness around the clock. As evidence of the relaxed attitude towards these drugs, though acknowledged over and over again by the primary sources referencing these events, not once did any investigators express any surprise as to the presence of the substances in the homes nor did they question as to how anyone could obtain such poisons.

Social Environment

It is, of course, general knowledge that women held a different role in the 19th century than they do today. It is no surprise then that many viewed marriage not just as the legal union between a man and woman in love, but also the only true form of social security for women.

In the seventeen women profiled in this book, many of them involved younger women marrying older men with some degree of property wealth. An inherited farm, some acres of land and a few hundred dollars would ensure a roof over a woman's head and food on her table.

Befitting of double-standards, while some questioned the motives of a younger woman marrying an older man, news of the contrary was received with the wink of an eye and comment as to the understandably appreciative attributes of the lady.

The collective perspective of the era might have been one of women as submissive in terms of social decorum. In isolated events, however, such as those we see here in these tales, it should not come as any great surprise that a woman stressed by factors beyond her control, when it came to personal survival, might, when no one is looking, make decisions beyond the norm to ensure her survival.

Psychological Factors

The psychology of child rearing most stands out in contrast to today. Today a child is the primary focus of the family. Parents invest the lion's share of their time, money and attention in the children, with the cost of raising a single child in the USA in 2014 to age 18 close to $250,000. And this number only demonstrates part of the difference. Marketing in the name of and directly to children is a multi-billion dollar business. One can discern with accuracy t that today's society is centered upon the rearing of children.

Well into the 19th century, however, children were still pretty much a commodity—produced to satisfy a family's need. More children meant more hands on the farm, and numbers grew a hedge against losing some offspring to early childhood diseases. At age 11, Fanny Scofield's parents "rented" her out to a neighboring family, either to save them the expense of housing and feeding her, or for some other form of compensation. It goes without say that she did not receive any formal education.

Unfortunately for newborns, the price of disposing of an unwanted baby amounted to less than $4. Mothers otherwise occupied didn't give a second thought to leaving their infants with unscrupulous baby farmers. Those who ran such unconscionable businesses possessed even fewer feelings for those children than the chicken farmer has for the hen whose neck he's wringing—

and they used much more egregious methods of disposal.

Mental health services just did not exist. Ella Holdridge exhibited the type of behavior that today would immediately result in psychological intervention. But even after murdering or attempting to murder more than seven children, authorities could only manage to house her in an orphanage, somewhat isolated and contained, but without affording the disturbed girl any treatment.

The Final Word

We can conclude that the psychosis of the female mind in the 1800's—or any time before, for that matter— does not differentiate from what it is today. Instead, as women over the last two centuries have increased their rights and freedoms within society, its corruption, dark influences, and temptations have infected them inherently in that interaction.

It is also interesting to note that the motivations of female serial killers, much more so than men, haven't really changed over the last 100 years. Contrary to men who focus on their victims according to a preselected profile and choose their subjects randomly, women on the other hand, tend to have a socially intimate relationship with their intended targets: husbands, lovers and even their own children. When it comes to the two genders, women and men respond to, and satisfy quite different needs.

Glossary

Black Widows

Black Widows are women who kill their husbands in most cases for material gain. The term is derived from the spider of the same name, which after mating with the smaller and weaker male kills and eats him. To be considered a black widow serial killer, a woman must murder no less than two husbands.

Black Widow is the category that covers most women serial killers. There are more than 30 cases recorded worldwide to date. Here in the United States, the most prolific include Elizabeth Routt, 1857, from Tennessee and Lulu Johnson from Oklahoma, 1899, who killed six husbands each. Margaret Summers, from Chicago around 1931, and Betty Neuman in 2008 both killed five husbands; Summers also killed 14 other people: a 3 year-old daughter, two nephews, her own brother and nine boarders. Daisy "Nanny" Doss, in 1954, killed four husbands and 7 others. No less than seven additional black widows, including Caroline Sorgenfrie, killed four husbands each.

Comfort killers may also fall into this category. Their motive is to ensure their current quality of life, even if that quality of life is neither luxurious nor wealthy. To do so, they remove anyone they deem a threat, such as an unfaithful or unhappy husband or even a child who is perceived as an obstacle to something else. The murder is often carried out by means that are less likely to arouse suspicion, such as poisoning and with a significant period of time between multiple acts.

Angels of Death

An angel of death is one who kills beneath the guise of providing health care to a person who is ill, but in reality is systematically killing that person. Angels of death are many a time driven by one of two motives. The first is sadistic, feeding off of the power over life and death. Stimulation comes from controlling a defenseless person and watching that individual suffer. The murder often occurs slowly over time. The second is a hero complex in which the angel of death endangers a person's life and then acts to remove the danger and thereby garners recognition as a savior. Motivation comes from the accolades and worship that is received from others in proximity to the setting. Munchausen Syndrome by Proxy is often mistaken as a similar motivation. However with MSP, the perpetrator is not acting as a hero, but themselves are desirous of the attention and sympathy that is given to parents of sick children. The murders are usually sudden and unexpected.

Two of the most notorious Angels of Death in history are Kristen Gilbert and Beverley Allitt. Gilbert, while working as a nurse in a VA hospital, killed no less than eight patients, by injecting them with epinephrine and causing massive heart attacks. Many believe she had a role in the death of more than 80 patients. Researchers think the attention of a male doctor motivated her.

Beverly Allitt hailed from England. Authorities accused her of murdering four children within the children's ward at the hospital in which she worked. She attempted the deaths of at least three others and caused bodily harm to six more. Though no one ever uncovered the motives for her actions, many people believe she suffered from Munchausen Syndrome and derived satisfaction from the sympathy she received in her role as the attending nurse.

Baby Farmers

The term *baby farming* was coined in Europe well before the practice became common place in the New World. According to a definition provided by the Department of Health in 1892, the practice involved women who were "receiving large numbers of children at a time and without proper accommodations for them."[1] Unheard of prior to the 1800s, the practice surfaced and grew in haste in urban areas like New York, Boston, Philadelphia and Baltimore. These areas

Glossary

exploded in population in the mid-19th century with the arrival of the working class and poor from Italy, Germany and Ireland, with the Five Points section of Lower Manhattan being the most infamous.

Unemployment, alcohol and the Civil War all contributed to men leaving behind or abandoning young mothers. Jobless and incapable of caring for the children they already had, these mothers took work which forced them from the home for long hours and paid poorly. Older children were left to run unsupervised in the streets, while infants were abandoned or "left" in the care of baby farmers for a fee.

Depending on the intent of the infant's mother, the fee would either be a onetime event or paid in payments. If the mother abandoned the baby, ostensibly for adoption, she intended the fee to cover the cost of care until the infant could be moved to a family. Women hired to breast feed infants, called wet nurses, provided nourishment. Unfortunately, many of these care providers were profiteers, interested only in the fee and not the child. If an adopting family could not be found for the child—if ever the intent—within a period of time deemed profitable by the baby farmer, they would leave the infant to starve or even murder the child outright and discard of the body.

Avengers

The serial killer motivated by revenge is striking out against those that have actually served or are perceived as an obstacle in the way of personal gain. The most notorious on record was Aileen Wournos. Born in 1956 in Michigan, her mother, who birthed her at only fourteen, soon abandoned Aileen and left her with non-nurturing grandparents. She claimed that her grandfather would obligate her to undress and then beat her. It is believed that around the age of eleven, a friend of her grandfathers raped and then routinely sexually abused her. At that age, also, she started exchanging sexual favors at school for material and monetary gain.

When Wournos grew to adulthood, she married a much older man. The marriage was soon after annulled as a result of larcenous and violent behavior. At the age of 30, she met and started a relationship with a younger waitress. As a means of supporting herself and her lover, she used prostitution to attract men, have them drive to a secluded area and then either before or during sex, kill them and discard of their bodies, stealing their cars, valuables and money. This she did no less than seven times. She was executed in 2002.

Question of Sanity

Killers of questionable sanity are motivated by mental disorders such as schizophrenia, delusions, paranoia or any other number of psychoses. These types of mental disorders sometimes result in dissociative behaviors in which the killer demonstrates a lack of empathy towards the victim. As a result, the killer is capable of inflicting pain and suffering, or taking life, without making any connection to the human condition, for example, putting herself in the place of the person she is killing.

References

Introduction

[1] March 16, 1892. "Brooklyn Castoffs." *Evening World*, p3. New York, New York.

Chapter 1

[1] June 18, 1894. "Lizzie Halliday's Case." *Indianapolis News*, p5. Indianapolis, Indiana.

[2] June 30, 1894. "Lizzie Halliday and Her Many Crimes." *Leavenworth Times*, p3. Leavenworth, Kansas.

[3] June 30, 1894. "Lizzie Halliday and Her Many Crimes." *Leavenworth Times*, p3. Leavenworth, Kansas.

[4] June 30, 1894. "Lizzie Halliday and Her Many Crimes." *Leavenworth Times*, p3. Leavenworth, Kansas.

[5] June 20, 1894. "Lizzie Halliday's Trial." *Middletown Daily Argus*, p5. Middletown, New York.

[6] http://unknownmisandry.blogspot.com/2011/09/serial-killer-lizzie-halliday-was-known.html

[7] October 4, 1906. "Mad Murderess Kills Girl Nurse." *French Broad Hustler*, p6. Hendersonville, North Carolina.

8 October 4, 1906. "Mad Murderess Kills Girl Nurse." *French Broad Hustler*, p6. Hendersonville, North Carolina.

9 August 21, 1895. "Lizzie Halliday Getting Better." *Middletown Daily Argus*, p7. Middletown, New York

10 September 28, 2006. "Murdered in an Insane Asylum." *Alexandria Gazette*, p1. Alexandria, Virginia.

11 June 29, 1918. "Lizzie Halliday Dies." *New York Times*, p20. New York, New York.

Chapter 2

1 Huntington, Willard V. 1891.*Oneonta Memories and Sundry Personal Recollections of the Author*, p40. The Bancroft Company, San Francisco.

2 http://www.newspapers.com/image/35908894/?terms=elizabeth+p.+mccraney. Correspondence of the *New York Tribune*. July 10, 1860.

Chapter 3

1 http://murderpedia.org/female.V/v/van-valkenburgh-elizabeth.htm

2 http://murderpedia.org.

3 http://murderpedia.org.

4 January 23, 1846. "Case of Mrs. Van Valkenburgh." *Brooklyn Daily Eagle*, p2. Brooklyn, New York.

Chapter 4

1 March 25, 1883. "The Haight Murder." *Times*, p1. Philadelphia, Pennsylvania.

2 February 26, 1884. "Warned by the Judge to Prepare for Death. –Nothing but the Governor's Clemency Can Save Her Now." *Ottawa Daily Republic*, p3. Ottawa, Kansas.

3 February 25, 1884. "Slain by His Aged Wife." *Delaware County Daily Times*, p1. Chester, Pennsylvania.

4 February 26, 1884. "Warned by the Judge to Prepare for Death. –Nothing but the Governor's Clemency Can Save Her Now." *Ottawa Daily Republic*, p3. Ottawa, Kansas.

References

[5] February 25, 1884. "An Aged Wife's Crime." *Chicago Daily Tribune*, p1. Chicago, Illinois.

[6] February 25, 1884. "An Aged Wife's Crime." *Chicago Daily Tribune*, p1. Chicago, Illinois

[7] http://www.jeffpaine.blogspot.com/2014/07/mrs-haight-of-deruyter-was-sentenced-to.html

[8] http://unknownmisandry.blogspot.com/2011/09/angenette-haight-black-widow-serial.html

Chapter 5

[1] http://www.co.genesee.ny.us/departments/history/genesee_county_history.html

[2] http://www.rootsweb.ancestry.com/-nycalaba/Polly.html

[3] http://unknownmisandry.blogspot.com/2011/09/mrs-frisch-new-york-state-serial-killer.html

[4] July 8, 1858. "Mrs. Polly Frisch…" *New York Tribune*, p3. New York, New York.

[5] December 17, 1892. "Polly Frisch a Free Woman." *The Cincinnati Enquirer*, p13. Cincinnati, Ohio

Chapter 6

[1] October 21, 1879. "A Startling Story." *Chicago Daily Tribune*, p2. Chicago, Illinois.

[2] October 23, 1879. "A Modern Borgia." *Reading Times*, p3. Reading, Pennsylvania.

[3] October 7, 1879. "The Chittenango Poisoning." *New York Times*, p5. New York, New York.

[4] October 7, 1879. "The Chittenango Poisoning." *New York Times*, p5. New York, NY.

Chapter 7

[1] *World, New York*, N.Y., June 8, 1891, p5

[2] *Wheeling Daily Intelligencer*, Wed., June 10, 1891

[3] *Salt Lake Tribune*, June 10, 1891, P1

[4] *Rome Semi-Weekly Citizen,* May 14, 1891,

Chapter 8

[1] July 2, 1876. *New York Times*, p8. New York, New York.

[2] July 2, 1876. *New York Times*, p8. New York, New York.

Chapter 9

[1] September 16, 1890. "Bodies of Dead Infants." *Scranton Republican*, p1. Scranton, Pennsylvania.

[2] IBID, *Scranton Republican*,

[3] October 7, 1890. "Baby Farmers Sentenced."

Chapter 10

[1] October 19, 1887. "The Babies Were Drugged." *Alton Evening Telegraph*, p1. Alton, Illinois.

[2] September 26, 1887. "Starved to Death." *Lebanon Daily News*, p1. Lebanon, Pennsylvania.

[3] October 1, 1887. "Cynthia McDonald…" *Daily Commonwealth*, p2. Topeka, Kansas.

[4] http://unknownmisandry.blogspot.com/2011/09/cynthia-mcdonald-child-care-provider.html

References

Chapter 11

[1] February 7, 1877. "Case of Alleged Baby Farming." *New York Times*, p8. New York, New York.

[2] February 7, 1877. "Horrible Trade: More Systematic Child Murder Brought to Light in New York." *Brooklyn Daily Eagle*, p4. Brooklyn, New York.

[3] February 7, 1877. "Horrible Trade."

[4] February 7, 1877. "Horrible Trade."

[5] February 7, 1877. "Horrible Trade."

[6] February 7, 1877. "Case of Alleged Baby Farming." *New York Times*, p8. New York, New York.

Chapter 12

[1] http://unknownmisandry.blogspot.com/2011/09/phebe-westlake-new-york-state-serial.html

[2] http://blogs.hudsonvalley.com/hudson-valley-history/2014/03/04/%e2%80%9ca-fiend-in-human-shape%e2%80%9d-chester%e2%80%99s-phebe-westlake/

[3] http://unknownmisandry.blogspot.com/2011/09/phebe-westlake-new-york-state-serial.html

[4] http://blogs.hudsonvalley.com/hudson-valley-history/2014/03/04/%e2%80%9ca-fiend-in-human-shape%e2%80%9d-chester%e2%80%99s-phebe-westlake/

[5] http://www.dartmouth.edu/~toxmetal/arsenic/history.html

Chapter 13

[1] http://history.rays-place.com/ny/mexico-ny.htm

[2] November 14, 1896. "Crime of a Little Girl." *San Francisco Call*, p3. San Francisco, California.

[3] November 14, 1896. "Crime of a Little Girl."

Chapter 14

[1] December 22, 1886. "Latest News." *Alton Evening Telegraph*, p1. Alton, Illinois.

[2] http://herkimer.nygenweb.net/warren/Drusemurder.html

[3] February 28, 1887. "The Woman's Confession." Lancaster Daily Intelligencer, p1. Lancaster, Pennsylvania.

[4] http://herkimer.nygenweb.net/warren/Drusemurder.html

[5] December 3, 1906. "Plans to Protect Gillette." *Sun,* p3. New York, New York.

[6] http://www.herkimer.nygenweb.net/warren/druseroxalana.html

Chapter 15

[1] http://en.wikipedia.org/wiki/Declaration_of_Sentiments

[2] http://www.murderpedia.org/female.A/a/antoine-mary.htm

Chapter 16

[1] July 20, 1892. "Young Borgia." *The Piqua Daily Call*, p5. Piqua, Ohio.

[2] July 20, 1892. "Young Borgia."

[3] http://unknownmisandry.blogspot.com/2013/07/ella-holdridge-funeral-loving-teenage.html

[4] July 20, 1892. "Young Borgia."

[5] July 20, 1892. "Young Borgia."

[6] July 20, 1892. "Young Borgia."

[7] http://www.sagepub.com/upm-data/19434_Section_I.pdf

References

Chapter 17

[1] August 27, 1847. "Murder—from the *Troy Budget*." *Brooklyn Daily Eagle*, p2. Brooklyn, New York.

[2] August 27, 1847. "Murder—from the *Troy Budget*."

[3] November 9, 1847. "A Woman Hung Today." *Brooklyn Daily Eagle*, p2. Brooklyn, New York.

[4] November 26, 1847. "From the Prisoner's Friend. A WOMAN HUNG." *Liberator*, p4. Boston, Massachusetts.

Index

Index

Index

Index

Index

Index

Index provided courtesy of Mary Pelletier-Hunyadi

Bibliography

Books

Hickey, Eric (2010). *Serial Murderers and their Victims*. Wadworth. ISBN 978-0-495-60081-7.

Holmes, Ronald M; Holmes, Stephen T (2000). *Mass murder in the United States*. Prentice Hall. ISBN 0-13-934308-3.

Howard, Amanda; Martin Smith (2004). *River of Blood: Serial Killers and Their Victims*. Universal. ISBN 978-1-58112-518-4.

Kelleher, Michael D.; Kelleher, C.L. (1998). *Murder Most Rare: The Female Serial Killer*. Westport, Connecticut: Praeger. ISBN 978-0-275-96003-2.Reynolds, Michael (2003). *Dead Ends: The Pursuit, Conviction and Execution of Female Serial Killer Aileen Wuornos, the Damsel of Death*. St. Martin's True Crime Library. ISBN 0-312-98418-9.

Russell, Sue (2002). *Lethal Intent: The Shocking True Story of One of America's Most Notorious Female Serial Killers*. Pinnacle. ISBN 0-7860-1518-7.

Vronsky, Peter (2007b). *Female Serial Killers: How and Why Women Become Monsters*. New York: Berkley Publishing Group.

Vronsky, Peter (2013). *"Serial Killer Zombie Apocalypse and the Dawn of the Less Dead: An Introduction to Sexual Serial Murder Today", in Serial Killers: True Crime Anthology 2014*. RJ Parker Publishing. ISBN 978-1494325893

Online Resources

Serial Killers

Differences between male and female serial killers http://brookeclukey.blogspot.com/2013/02/female-vs-male-serial-killers.html

Gender Differences Between Male and Female Serial Killers http://kheide.myweb.usf.edu/file/journal/gender.pdf

What motivates female serial killers. http://www.psychologytoday.com/blog/wicked-deeds/201501/what-motivates-female-serial-killers

5 myths about serial killers http://www.scientificamerican.com/article/5-myths-about-serial-killers-and-why-they-persist-excerpt/

Serial Killer Statistics http://maamodt.asp.radford.edu/Serial%20Killer%20Information%20Center/Serial%20Killer%20Statistics.pdf

Historical

History of Chenango and Madison counties www.usgenweb.info/nychenango/books/1880hist.htm

History of Erie County, New York http://history.rays-place.com/ny/cty-erie.htm

History of Fulton County, New York http://www.schenectadyhistory.org/local/fulton-history.html

History of Genesee County New York http://history.rays-place.com/ny/cty-genesee.htm

History of George Eastman and Family http://www.notablebiographies.com/Du-Fi/Eastman-George.htmlhttp://

History of Herkimer County New York http://history.rays-place.com/ny/herk-herkimer.htm

History of Long Island http://en.wikipedia.org/wiki/History_of_Long_Island

History of Monroe County New York http://en.wikipedia.org/wiki/Rochester,_New_York

History of Montgomery County New York http://en.wikipedia.org/wiki/Montgomery_County,_New_York

History of New York City A brief history of nyc http://www.localhistories.org/newyork.htm

Bibliography

History of Oneida County New York http://en.wikipedia.org/wiki/Oneida_County,_New_York

History of Orange County New York http://www.orangecountygov.com content/11html

History of Oswego County New York http://history.rays-place.com/ny/cty Oswego.

History of Otsego County New York http://external.oneonta.edu/cooper/articles/nyhistory/1954nyhistory-butterfield.html

History of Rochester, New York http://www.libraryweb.org/~rochhist/indexa.htm

History of Sullivan County New York genealogytrails.com/ny/sullivan/history.html56/

About the Author

Michael Keene worked for twenty-five years in the financial services industry as a financial advisor. He is the author of *Folklore and Legends of Rochester, The Mystery of Hoodoo Corner; Murder, Mayhem and Madness, 150 Years of Crime and Punishment in Western New York; Mad~House, The Hidden History of Insane Asylums in 19th Century New York;* and *Abandoned, The Untold Story of Orphan Asylums.* He is also the producer of the award-winning documentary series, *Visions, True Stories of Spiritualism, Secret Societies & Murder.* He lives in Pittsford, New York with his wife Diana and their daughter Michele, and grandson, Joshua. His website address is http://www.ad-hoc-productions.com and email is: info@ad-hoc-visions.com

CPSIA information can be obtained at www.ICGtesting.com
Printed in the USA
BVOW08s0443230215

388866BV00003B/3/P